YORK NOTES

General Editors: Professor A.N. Jeffares (*University of Stirling*) & Professor Suheil Bushrui (*American University of Beirut*)

T.S. Eliot

THE
WASTE LAND

Notes by Alasdair D.F. Macrae

MA (EDINBURGH) *Lecturer in English Studies*
University of Stirling

LONGMAN
YORK PRESS

YORK PRESS
Immeuble Esseily, Place Riad Solh, Beirut.

LONGMAN GROUP LIMITED
Longman House, Burnt Mill,
Harlow, Essex CM20 2JE, England
and Associated companies throughout the world

© Librairie du Liban 1980

First published 1980
Second impression 1984
ISBN 0 582 78212 0
Printed in Hong Kong by
Sing Cheong Printing Co Ltd

Contents

Part 1

Introduction

Life of T. S. Eliot

Thomas Stearns Eliot was born in 1888 in Missouri in the United States of America. His father's family traced their ancestors back to immigrants to New England from East Coker, Somerset, in England in the seventeenth century. Eliot's parents were prosperous and cultured and they ensured that he received an excellent education. At Harvard University, where he studied philosophy between 1906 and 1914, Eliot developed an interest in the medieval Italian poet Dante and the nineteenth century French poets, particularly Baudelaire and Laforgue, and wrote his first significant poems. 'The Love Song of J. Alfred Prufrock', written in 1910–1911, was to be the title poem of his first collection of poems published in 1917.

He travelled and studied in France, Germany and England and in 1915 settled in London. After his marriage to an English girl, Vivien Haig-Wood, he worked for a couple of years as a schoolteacher before he obtained a position in Lloyd's Bank. After serving as assistant editor of *The Egoist*, Eliot worked as editor of *The Criterion* from 1922 to 1939; both were influential literary magazines. His second collection of verse, *Poems*, also known as *Ara Vos Prec*, was published in 1920, the date of his first collection of critical essays, *The Sacred Wood*.

Eliot's marriage was not happy and his health deteriorated to such a degree that he had to take an extended holiday first in Margate on the South Coast and then in Lausanne in Switzerland. It was during this period that he composed *The Waste Land*, first published in the October 1922 issue of *The Criterion*. In the 1920s Eliot wrote many of his most influential critical essays, particularly on English seventeenth-century literature. *The Hollow Men* appeared in 1925 and by 1930 Eliot had completed *Ash Wednesday* and the *Ariel Poems*. In 1927 Eliot became a British citizen and in 1928 he described his point of view as 'classicist in literature, royalist in politics, and anglo-catholic in religion.' From 1925 till his death, Eliot worked as a director of the publishing company now known as Faber and Faber.

After an absence of seventeen years, Eliot visited the United States to deliver at Harvard University lectures published in 1933 as *The Use of*

Poetry and the Use of Criticism. In the following year Eliot's pageant play *The Rock* was performed in London. His interest in drama, earlier manifested in the unfinished *Sweeney Agonistes* (1927), developed in the later part of his writing career and produced five verse plays between 1935 and 1958. *Murder in the Cathedral*, examining the martyrdom of Thomas à Becket, is concerned with similar religious themes to those of *Ash Wednesday*. In *The Family Reunion* (1939), Eliot moves into his contemporary world. The later three plays *The Cocktail Party* (1949), *The Confidential Clerk* (1953), and *The Elder Statesman* (1958), all received their premieres at the Edinburgh Festival and enjoyed considerable commercial success.

In 1935, the year of *Murder in the Cathedral*, Eliot published 'Burnt Norton', the first of his *Four Quartets*, eventually to be completed in 1942. His later work is less cluttered with literary references and demonstrates Eliot's wish to write for a larger audience than that of *The Waste Land*. After 1942 Eliot wrote no poems of significance. The Order of Merit and the Nobel Prize were awarded to him in 1948. In that same year his wife, long since separated from him, died, and in 1957 Eliot married Valerie Fletcher, his secretary. Despite ill health during the final fifteen years of his life, Eliot was able to travel and deliver lectures and his last few years were among his happiest. He died in January 1965 at the age of 76.

Intellectual background

While at Harvard, Eliot was influenced by the philosopher George Santayana (1863–1952) and the critic Irving Babbitt (1865–1933) who both stressed a need for intellectual self-discipline and the inter-relationship of literary and social values. Santayana and Babbit could be described as conservative thinkers whereas the British philosopher, F.H. Bradley (1846–1924), the subject of Eliot's doctoral research, was part of a new movement questioning many of the assumptions of nineteenth-century thought. Bradley's *Appearance and Reality* was first published in 1893; in it Bradley declared that most of our statements about the world are 'riddled with contradictions' because we are describing appearance and not reality. When we devise a scientific theory or seek to describe God and the nature of the self we are, according to Bradley, acting without a clear understanding of how the mind perceives the world.

Bradley's challenge formed part of a series of new theories and questions which forced a re-appraisal of traditional attitudes. Back in 1848, Karl Marx (1819–93) and Friedrich Engels (1820–95) had published

The Communist Manifesto, an analysis of the development of society which emphasised the economic forces which shape social change and the struggle of classes for power. Their attack on what Marx and Engels called capitalist society was not widely supported but, over the following hundred years, Marx's theories and method of social analysis have exerted an enormous influence on the way we think about society and the individual. Furthermore, Marx's view of history is secular and materialistic; as such, it is inevitably in direct conflict with religious belief.

Charles Darwin's (1809–82) book *On the Origin of Species by means of Natural Selection* appeared in 1859 and offered new evidence in support of an argument challenging the literal truth of the biblical account of man's development. Darwin's evolutionary theory suggested that man was not created suddenly but was the result of a long development from more primitive forms. Man, like other animals, adapts, or is adapted, to function more satisfactorily in an environment. Both Marx's theory of social change, what he called the dialectic, and Darwin's theory of biological evolution shared the idea that man was advancing to a better life.

Sigmund Freud (1856–1939), whose work in psycho-analysis began in the 1890s, was fascinated by the primitive in man, whether in so-called primitive societies or in the unconscious part of the mind. His important work *The Interpretation of Dreams* appeared in 1899. According to Freud, human behaviour is seldom the result of a rational decision but derives from the pressures of our unconscious impulses and fears. Sexual anxiety and the wish for sexual gratification constitute the most dominating force of our lives; our actions are often disguised expressions of this force. In the imagery of dreams, myths and literature Freud saw the symbolic manifestation of our sexual problems. Throughout his long career, till his death in 1939, Freud conceded that what he was analysing had always been presented by artists but certainly no thinker of the past hundred years has had a more powerful effect on the writer's view of his own work. Freud's one-time colleague, Carl Gustav Jung (1875–1961), saw not sex but a series of mythic patterns, the imprint of the central experiences of mankind, as the basis of our conception of the world. Jung believed that modern man inherited a store of these mythic patterns, the collective unconscious, and that the artist is a person particularly gifted in bringing these unconscious images, archetypes, to the surface. Freud seemed to see all art as an expression of the artist's disorder, his neurosis; Jung saw the artist as the image-maker and spiritual explorer for his audience.

Jung and Freud each acknowledged a huge debt to the anthropologist, Sir James Frazer (1854-1941), whose monumental study of primitive ritual and myth, *The Golden Bough*, was published between 1890 and 1915. Frazer's book suggests that no human practice is unique but is one form of response to our shared situation and the similarities between civilised and primitive cultures, between Christianity and pagan religions, are more marked and significant than any contrasts. The idea that human truth and morality make sense in the perspective of a particular tribe and are, therefore, relative has something in common with the theory of relativity worked out for the physical world by the physicist Albert Einstein (1879-1955) at exactly the same period.

This was the period leading up to the First World War (1914-1918) in which the European countries which had grown in power during the nineteenth century engaged in a costly and futile struggle. No country emerged from the war stronger or richer, and the main effects of the conflict were a disenchantment with any glib optimism as to the improvement of mankind and a search for some ideology to cope with the economic and political problems of Europe. In 1917 the Russian Revolution under Vladimir Ilyich Lenin (1870-1924) took place and during the early 1920s there was a rapid strengthening of Communist and Fascist parties throughout Europe. The Fascist party led by Benito Mussolini (1883-1945) came to power in Italy in 1922. The basic theoretical difference was that Communism claimed to be government by the people and Fascism claimed that leadership should be given to the people by a select group of talented men. In practice both systems seemed to rely on a rigid and exclusive party totally responsible for planning, freedom and justice and both used the army and police to impose a dictatorial system. Artists throughout Europe felt obliged to take sides and many of the major English-speaking writers—W.B. Yeats (1865-1939), Ezra Pound (1885-1972), T.S. Eliot (1888-1965), P. Wyndham Lewis (1884-1957) and D.H. Lawrence (1885-1930)—initially showed sympathy for the Right (the Fascists) against the Left.

A result of the First World War was the break-up of the Austro-Hungarian Empire and its mixture of nationalities and languages. The old aristocratic splendour of Vienna was becoming a thing of the past. It was in the context of this political and ethnic confusion that the German Nazis were later to insist on their idea of racial purity.

Britain, too, was seriously weakened by the war. By the end of the war she had nine million of her citizens in the armed forces and the munitions works; she, with her allies from the British Empire, had lost over a million men in the fighting. The Empire itself, the largest the world has seen, was beginning to break apart: there was bitter discontent in parts as separated as South Africa, Ireland, India and Egypt. In the 1920s the unemployment level rose and many people were forced to live in abject poverty. Over the previous fifty years the provision of education and the organisation of trade unions had improved but it seemed almost impossible for anyone to see a solution to the appalling economic situation after the war. During the nineteenth century there had been a large movement of the British population away from the land and into the rapidly expanding industrial towns. By the 1920s all the major towns and cities had developed areas of slum conditions. Engines and machines of every sort appeared to be dominating the lives of ordinary people; the people felt that they were becoming parts of a mechanical process. To add to this feeling of helplessness a rigid class system maintained a system of privilege, snobbery and distrust.

It is curious that such a dismal period should now be referred to as the Roaring Twenties but people did make a hectic attempt to enjoy themselves and to break down the stiff attitudes of Victorian times. Moral codes, traditional Christianity, the roles of the sexes, all were challenged and some prominent people made a virtue of shocking and sensational behaviour. The development of radio and film and new, faster methods of travel allowed celebrities to enjoy a previously unprecedented international fame. Newspapers with mass circulations appeared to cultivate in their readers a taste for sensationalism and vulgarity and the most tragic and serious situations were trivialised to cater for this appetite.

The dilemma of America and Europe was one of belief. The seeming solidity of the social class system and orthodox Christian faith so apparent in many aspects of nineteenth-century life was now demonstrated to be inadequate. Friedrich Wilhelm Nietzsche (1844–1900), the German philosopher, had proclaimed that God was dead, but the final ten years of his own life till his death in 1900 were spent in physical and mental paralysis. His crude assertion and his paralysis seem deeply symptomatic of intellectual life at the turn of the century. Western men had exhausted their spiritual supplies; some rushed around looking for replacements in magic, other religions, science, a life of sensations through drugs, sex and excitement, and others claimed that despair was the only honest response to a chaotic universe.

T.S. Eliot, having come from a traditionally-minded American background but led by his interests, friendships and reading into the perplexities of the intellectual scene, had to work out his own scheme of beliefs in relation to his personal experiences and the nature of the world around him.

Literary background

In the second half of the nineteenth century there were two main movements in European literature: Realism and Symbolism. The Realist
writers aimed to present man as a social creature and to lay bare the
processes by which economic and political pressures affect man's behaviour. In style, the Realists sought simplicity, directness, and avoided
ornament; accurate representation of a social situation was all important and because of their reformist ideals they often concentrated on the
abuses and nastiness in the hope that their readers would feel persuaded to change society. A weakness in the Realist writings was the
absence of imagination: everything was spelled out clearly and there
was little to delight or excite the reader's intellect. This discouragement
of imagination, added to the solid social concern, helps to explain why
Realism had little following among poets and was primarily a movement of novelists and dramatists. It could be argued, however, that
Realism did help to make some poets more aware of social issues and of
a responsibility to their readers, and Walt Whitman (1819–92), the
American poet, achieved international fame as a poet of democracy,
the working man and colloquial language.

Symbolist writing, on the other hand, was indirect, allusive, often
obscure, and tended to concentrate on evoking individual moods and
elusive states of mind. The major early Symbolist poets were French:
Charles Baudelaire (1821–1867), Paul Verlaine (1844–1896), Arthur
Rimbaud (1854–1891), Jules Laforgue (1860–1887) and Stéphane
Mallarmé (1842–1898); but their work was not widely known in Britain
and America till Arthur Symons (1865–1945) published *The Symbolist
Movement in Literature* in 1899. Although these poets often had very
decided views on society, the concentration of their poetry was on the
processes of their own minds, and fastidious attention was paid to form
and language. Words and images were so chosen and arranged as to set
up a complex criss-crossing of associations and the reader could delight
in exploring this endless maze. Parallel to the Realists' emphasis on
social injustice and constriction, the Symbolists often stressed moods of
disappointment, pain, guilt and loneliness. In Baudelaire and Laforgue,
however (the Symbolists who exerted the strongest influence on Eliot),
there is a sense of humour, a mocking self-awareness that helps to
balance the private, melancholy quality. Furthermore, in these two
poets there is an acute interest in the position of a sensitive, individual
artist in a vulgar, materialistic society. In Baudelaire, more than in any
other European poet before him, we are made aware of the city with its
variety, its crowds, its mechanical cruelty, its excitement, its horror.

In 1908, T.S. Eliot read Symons's *The Symbolist Movement in Literature* and was introduced through it to a kind of poetry that was not being written at that time in America. Curiously enough, one of the major influences on Baudelaire had been the American writer Edgar Allan Poe (1809–49), but Eliot, in his early years, seemed determined to look beyond America for his models and even recent English literature was largely bypassed by him. Robert Browning (1812–89) was an exception to this neglect of English poets and his use of colloquial language and the dramatic monologue both influenced Eliot's development. A dramatic monologue is a poem in which we hear the words and thoughts of a character in a situation; the character is not straightforwardly the author, he is a dramatic invention of the author.

While he was a student at Harvard, Eliot came to know the work of Dante Alighieri (1265–1321), a poet whom he was later to see as the major guide and model for his own poetry. What Eliot particularly admired in the medieval Italian poet were the directness and economy of his language and the width of emotional experience, especially in the scenes of Hell, Purgatory and Paradise in *The Divine Comedy*. Dante as a figure is present throughout *The Divine Comedy* but, according to Eliot, the reader is not burdened with, or embarrassed by, Dante's private pains or pleasures. Eliot felt that Dante's restraint, his balance between the personal and the impersonal, had much to do with Dante belonging to a tradition of writing and thinking.

During his first ten years in Europe, Eliot spent much of his time considering what he meant by a tradition and attempting to define the tradition of which he felt a part. In 1914 he first met his fellow American poet, Ezra Pound, and they discovered that their poetic interests and aims were very similar. Pound became an indefatigable helper of Eliot, providing him with encouragement, helpful criticism, new ideas, publicity and literary contacts and he made himself responsible for finding publishers for Eliot's poetry. Pound's early poetry, before his major work *The Cantos*, is characterised by a variety of verse forms adapted from many languages and periods. Much of his best work took the form of translations or, more properly, imitations of Classical, medieval Italian and Provençal and Chinese poems. Both Eliot and Pound had learned in their university training to value the achievements of earlier cultural periods and both had developed a gift for selecting a poem, an incident, a person, quintessential to that period. *The Cantos* (1917–1969) is Pound's attempt to organise these selections from world history into a vast scheme which could provide an aesthetic, moral and political education for his own generation.

For several years before he met Eliot, Pound was one of the leading members of the Imagist group. The Imagists felt that poetry in English had become tired, repetitive and habit-bound; they urged the need for freedom of subject matter, concentration of statement, originality of poetic image and the use of a verse free from rigid rules of rhyme and metre. Eliot never belonged to the group but he shared many of their original aims. Self-discipline, understatement, the inseparability of form and content were admired by him as classical virtues and he attacked the expression of unconsidered emotion in stale language that he associated with the romantic tradition in English poetry.

Many people would now accept the assessment voiced by Eliot and Pound that English poetry of the late nineteenth and early twentieth centuries lacked vitality and intellectual rigour. Looking back through the history of English literature for these missing qualities, Eliot found them most notably in the work of the poets and dramatists of the first half of the seventeenth century. In Shakespeare, the group of poets called the Metaphysical Poets, particularly John Donne (1572–1631), and the Jacobean playwrights, Eliot discovered a blend of emotion and thought, immediacy and technical control which, he felt, provided a helpful example for twentieth-century poets like himself. According to Eliot, a split between thought and feeling, what he called a 'dissociation of sensibility', occurred in English poetry about the time of John Milton (1608–74) and this split enfeebled nearly all subsequent poets. Before this split took place, writers saw life whole and the range of vocabulary in their work reflected the width of this experience and learning; to be intellectually challenging was for them a virtue and they expected their readers to enjoy struggling with unusual images, startling juxtapositions, irony and obliqueness.

Pound and Eliot's questioning of contemporary literary values, their search for worthwhile models, their experiments with verse, are all part of a wider European and American development known as Modernism. Modernism comprises many divergent theories and movement but all these are characterised by an overthrow of artistic conventions. For many members of the public, these movements in music, the visual arts and literature were not experiments or developments but were insults to the very idea of art. There were riots in theatres, art galleries and concert halls; charges of obscenity, irreverence and sensationalism were levelled against the artists and writers. In 1907 Pablo Picasso (1881–1973) completed his controversial painting *Les Demoiselles d'Avignon* (The Young Ladies of Avignon). In it the conventional subject of the female nude is dislocated into an arrangement of angular shapes and harsh colours and the faces of several of the young ladies are strongly reminiscent of tribal masks. The result is that the picture can be viewed in different ways: as a variation on a common subject of painting; as a play on geometric patterns; as a cultural or social comment suggesting that behind the present lies the mythic or the primitive. Picasso's development lay through Cubism which stressed a formalist, abstract element in art, to a collage technique in which various materials and bits and pieces like bottles or metals could be incorporated into a painting in such a way that the traditional gap between the artificial and the actual could be bridged.

The musical event, parallel in its shock effect to Picasso's *Les Demoiselles d'Avignon*, was the performance in 1913 of *The Rite of Spring*, a ballet by Igor Stravinsky (1882–1971). Harsh, strident dissonances interrupted any harmonies and, as in Picasso's composition, the introduction of African-sounding material suggested to the audience a struggle between disorder and order. Eliot saw the ballet performed in London in 1921 and, although he considered that the dancing was not a total success, he felt that the music metamorphosed 'the rhythm of the steppes into the scream of the motor horn, the rattle of machinery, the grind of wheels, the beating of iron and steel, the roar of the underground railway, and the other barbaric cries of modern life'. It is apparent that Eliot was impressed not by a clash between ancient ritual and myth and modern behaviour but by a sense of continuity in man's search for significance. What was new in Stravinsky was not the presence of ancient myths—Richard Wagner (1813–83) had based his operas on Germanic myths and legends—but the setting of the myth in a modern context and expressed in a modern musical idiom.

Eliot saw that modern life could be interpreted and could gain depth of meaning by being allied to parallel patterns of human behaviour embodied in myth and legend. This idea he saw realised in the work of two of the most distinguished contemporary writers, W.B. Yeats and James Joyce (1882–1941), both Irish. In terms of influence on Eliot's *The Waste Land*, Joyce was the more immediately important figure, so important, indeed, that Eliot told him, 'I wish, for my own sake, that I had not read it'. The 'it' was Joyce's *Ulysses*, eventually published in Paris in 1922 but parts of which Eliot had been reading as early as 1918. Eliot had come to know Joyce through their mutual friend, Ezra Pound. In *Ulysses*, a single day (16 June, 1904) in the life of Leopold Bloom is presented in detail against a framework of the episodes in the wanderings of Odysseus (Ulysses) in the Greek epic, *The Odyssey*. In its contemporary detail, the novel is highly naturalistic while in its richness of association and cross-reference and in the density of the language it is a Symbolist work. Joyce varies the prose style in the different episodes of his novel, ranging from the colloquial to the sophisticated, from passages of dialogue to an unpunctuated stream of consciousness; to describe the style is to offer a catalogue of the experiments in modern literature. In his review of *Ulysses*, Eliot wrote: 'I hold this book to be the most important expression which the present age has found . . . In using the myth, in manipulating a continuous parallel between contemporaneity and antiquity, Mr Joyce is pursuing a method which others must pursue after him . . . It is simply a way of controlling, of ordering, of giving a shape and significance to the intense panorama of futility and anarchy which is contemporary history.'

A note on the text

Towards the end of 1919, Eliot said in a letter to his mother that he was about to start on a long poem. During the years 1919–1922 Eliot was overworked, his health was bad, his wife was mentally and physically ill, their marriage was painful to both of them, they were constantly short of money and the future looked bleak. Eliot could not find the time necessary to concentrate on a long poem but in the autumn of 1921 he was given leave from his job to visit a psychologist in Switzerland.

By January 1922, Eliot had handed over to Pound what he had written while abroad. The final poem as published in October 1922 was very markedly the result of the collaboration between the two poets. The main effects of Pound's suggestions were to tighten the organisation of the poem and to remove some overwritten satirical sketches and personal elements. Eliot was also advised by Pound against using his earlier poem *Gerontion* as a prelude to *The Waste Land*.

The notes which now accompany the poem were not part of Eliot's original plan and were not present with the first publication. When the New York publishing company, Boni and Liveright, accepted the poem for publication in book form, they asked him to add some material to make up the size of a small book. Later in his life, Eliot came to regret the inclusion of the notes because he felt that they distracted readers' attention from the poem itself, but he did not have them removed.

When the poem was published Eliot presented the manuscripts and typescripts with his and Pound's revisions as a gift to John Quinn (1870–1924), a New York lawyer. On Quinn's death in 1924 the manuscripts disappeared and speculation as to their contents and their fate continued until 1968, when, to everyone's amazement, they were discovered in the New York Public Library. Eliot's widow Valerie prepared a transcript of the original sheets; this was published by Faber in 1971.

Part 2

Summaries
of THE WASTE LAND

A general summary

Except in the case of narrative poems, it is extremely difficult to sum-
marise a poem in a way that is fair to the nature of the poem. Because of
its organisation (see the section on Structure, page 49), *The Waste Land*
resists the very idea of a summary. Nonetheless, like any other object, it
can be described and even a crude summary may help to indicate the
general shape of the poem.

In Part I, 'The Burial of the Dead', Eliot conveys a sense of apprehension and incomprehension in various characters presented in different
situations. The lack of understanding is not helped by Madame
Sosostris, a fortune-teller, whose enigmatic pronouncements only make
sense later in the poem. The city, in particular London, is a grim place of
people unable to live fully or see a way out of their deadness.

Part II, 'A Game of Chess', offers two scenes showing the essential
emptiness of people's lives. The first presents in a lavishly decorated
room a rich lady whose constant questions express her anxiety and lack
of control. The second scene is set in a London pub where two women
discuss the predicament in which Lil finds herself.

The theme of sexual dissatisfaction is explored in Part III, 'The Fire
Sermon', where Eliot, ranging about in time from Buddha and St
Augustine to the present day, shows how man's aspirations to a higher,
more spiritual mode of living are constantly thwarted by his subservi-
ence to his bodily appetites and his self-centredness.

In the brief Part IV, 'Death by Water', a drowned merchant's body
decomposes in the sea. He seems to have achieved nothing.

Part V, 'What the Thunder said', begins with a description of the
death of Jesus and goes on to relate a gruelling journey through the
desert to an empty chapel. The traveller has to suffer hardships, delusions and a sense that all is chaotic and meaningless before he arrives. In
the final section of the poem the arrival of rain is intimated and the
voice of the thunder offers three words of advice: 'give', 'sympathise',
and 'control'. At the very end these words are set alongside various
phrases which echo themes and motifs which have appeared earlier in
the poem.

Detailed summaries

The title

Eliot, in his preliminary note to the poem, acknowledges his indebtedness to two works: *The Golden Bough* (1890–1915) by Sir James Frazer and *From Ritual to Romance* (1920) by Jessie L. Weston. The part of Frazer's work which particularly excited Eliot is concerned with the myths associated with Adonis, Osiris and Attis. These deities were seen by successive civilisations in the Eastern Mediterranean and the Middle East as the powers of nature and, each year, ceremonies were performed in their honour to ensure the return of spring and the fertility of the crops. Water is essential for fertility; without water, in rain or river, the land and the people die. Following Frazer, Jessie Weston showed that the rituals and myths associated with these deities did not die out on the arrival of Christianity but were incorporated into the material of literature in medieval Europe. In particular, she traced the legend of the Holy Grail in the chivalric romances. The Grail of the story was the cup used by Christ at his last supper with his disciples and later used to catch the dripping blood from his crucified body. It was believed that this sacred relic was brought to Glastonbury in England before being lost. The search for the lost Grail was symbolic of man's search for truth. The questing knight of the romances had to journey to the Chapel Perilous and there learn to ask the right questions concerning the Grail and the Lance which had pierced Christ's side on the Cross.

The cup and spear also carry a sexual symbolism of the female and male elements necessary for regeneration. This overlapping of the spiritual and the physical is contained in the figure who lies behind the questing knight. The Fisher King is the sexually wounded ruler of a country which has itself become infertile and the search for the Grail is undertaken by his knight to restore life to his kingdom. Jessie Weston saw in the title, the Fisher King, a definite connection between the fish as representative of the basic water of all life and the fish symbol so closely associated with the early Christian Church. The myth of the impotent ruler, the waste land and the quest for a regenerative power appears in many forms in literature: for example, in *Oedipus Rex* by the Greek dramatist Sophocles (496–405 BC); *Morte d'Arthur* by Sir Thomas Malory (1400–1471), and *Idylls of the King* by Lord Alfred Tennyson (1809–92). Wagner's operas, particularly *Parsifal*, were also demonstrations to Eliot of how such myth material could be used in a modern artistic idiom.

From the manuscript of the poem, it appears that the title *The Waste*

Land was a later thought. Large sections of what developed into the poem were grouped under the title, 'He Do the Police in Different Voices', a quotation from *Our Mutual Friend* (1864-5), the novel by Charles Dickens (1812-70), but, although it suited the scenes of social comedy in the early drafts, such a title would have been totally unsatisfactory for the poem that emerged. For Eliot the waste land is that area of human life where men exist without a guiding faith, where men have turned their backs on spiritual enlightenment, and the present title points to this dilemma.

Epigraph*

   'For I saw with my own eyes the Sybil
of Cumae hanging in a cage and the boys were
talking to her: "What do you want, Sybil?"
She answered, "I want to die"'.

The Sybil was a Greek prophetess who, when consulted by people for her advice, gave enigmatic answers. She appealed to the God Apollo to grant her as many years of life as she had grains of sand in her hand. Her wish was granted. She became older and older, more and more feeble, but she could not die. Life came to be an agony of boredom and she was tormented by groups of boys teasing her with their questions. The quotation comes from *The Satyricon* by Petronius, an author (first century AD) of the later Roman Empire who wrote about the vulgarity and decadence of the period. This story concerning the holy Sybil is presented among other inconsequential incidents at a debauched banquet.

   Eliot had intended to use as an epigraph the words 'The horror! The horror!' from the story *Heart of Darkness* by the Polish-born English novelist Joseph Conrad (1857-1924), but was dissuaded by Ezra Pound. Both the chosen and the discarded quotations suggest a vision of moral emptiness on the part of their original speakers; life has lost all its charm and death can only be a welcome release for the sufferer. The Sybil is related to the other prophetic figures in the poem, Madame Sosostris and Tiresias.

The dedication

NOTES AND GLOSSARY:

Ezra Pound: (1885-1972), American poet and close friend of Eliot (see pages 11, 12 and 14)

* Short quotation used to preface a work

il miglior fabbro: (*Italian*) 'the better craftsman'. Dante (*Purgatory* xxvi, 117) applauded the mastery of the Provençal poet, Arnaut Daniel, with these words. Eliot added the dedication to his poem in 1923 in gratitude to Ezra Pound for his help in shaping *The Waste Land* (see page 14) and in appreciation of Pound's skill as a poet

I. The Burial of the Dead

The title of Part I, 'The Burial of the Dead', intimates the central concern of the whole poem as well as of Part I. What do we mean by 'life' and 'death'? Each religion, in its ceremonies concerning the dead, gives some particular answer to the question. Many of these religious answers rest on a belief in the possibility of resurrection or the contribution of the dead to the replenishing and perpetuation of life. In Christian terms, the sacrificial death of Jesus Christ, the God-man, is essential to the well-being of the world. In the non-Christian terms examined by James Frazer, the idea of sacrifice for the welfare of the tribe was extremely wide-spread.

Part I can be examined most easily by accepting Eliot's division of the seventy-six lines into four paragraphs or sections. Eliot's method requires that we move from section to section without looking for a kind of narrative continuity which he does not use; nor does he explain to us where he is going or what he is attempting to achieve. We must allow a pattern to emerge in our own minds.

In the first paragraph (lines 1–18), there are two units: lines 1–7 and lines 8–18. The two units overlap but, basically, the first is vegetal in emphasis and the second is social. The opening statement sounds paradoxical in that the month of April is traditionally seen in England as the first month of spring, gentle after the harshness of winter. Eliot seems to recall the opening lines of Geoffrey Chaucer's (1340–1400) General Prologue to *The Canterbury Tales:*

Whan that Aprille with his shoures sote (sweet)
The droghte of Marche hath perced to the rote . . .
Than longen folk to goon on pilgrimages.

Eliot's poem, too, is concerned with a kind of pilgrimage or quest but, at the start of his poem, the traditional signal does not prompt the inhabitants of the 'dead land' to thoughts of hope and departure, quite the reverse. Winter is seen as the comfortable season, maintaining as it had done a minimal life where action was not called for. The arrival of

April is an agony to the speakers because it makes demands of them and reminds them of past and future ('memory and desire'). The lilacs of line 2 occur elsewhere in Eliot's work as suggesting powerful emotion and tenderness (see his poem 'Portrait of a Lady') and in the waste land emotion must be avoided. The main imagery of these lines is of vegetable life and the verbs in the present participle ('breeding', 'mixing', 'stirring', 'covering', 'feeding') emphasise a lack of motion.

The progression of the seasons continues in line 8 but the 'us' are now more human, existing in a world of parks and cafés. Among the smart people going round the fashionable places in Europe there is an anxiousness communicated in the abrupt shifts in the syntax of the speaker and in the restless movement from place to place. This is the Central Europe of the period around the First World War when the traditional aristocratic patterns and national boundaries were breaking up. The insistence by the Countess Marie that she is not Russian is possibly a reaction to the Communist Revolution in Russia in 1917 and a clinging to what she considers to be a more civilised nationality. The nervous, rootless mentality looks forward to the conversation of the rich woman in Part II.

Like the first paragraph, the second (lines 19–42) can be divided into two units. In the first of these units (lines 19–30), Eliot adopts a language strongly reminiscent of the prophetic books of the Old Testament. Just as the prophet Ezekiel was taken to the valley strewn with the bones of the dead and asked, 'Son of man, can these bones live?' so we are asked what life can come out of the wilderness of our world. Because we are spiritually dead we can envisage no possibilities but the unending routine of our journey through the desert of our days. What we must learn to understand is our condition of mortality, the fact of death and our present helplessness. The Cumaean Sybil of the epigraph asked for unending life; she was granted her wish and her handful of dust became a rebuke to her:

The two questions from Wagner's opera provide a frame for the episode concerning the hyacinth girl. The story of Tristan and Isolde is one of the world's great love stories. The first quotation comes from the beginning of Wagner's opera on the subject; a sailor longs for his loved one. Later in the story the same words could be used by the wounded Tristan when he hopes for the arrival of Isolde from Ireland. His lookout on the sea cliffs tells him that there is no sign of her. His urgent hopes are disappointed and when she does eventually arrive the strain is too much for Tristan and he dies. In between the anticipation and disappointment of Tristan's love are set the anticipation and bewilderment of the lover of the hyacinth girl. The moment of intensity, of ecstasy, was built up to but, at the very point when everything hoped for should have been realised, he had frozen and his vision had shown him what Tristan had experienced, the emptiness and futility of his love.

Throughout the poem various prophetic figures appear, including the Sybil, Ezekiel, Tiresias, the Buddha, and the thunder of the final part. Madame Sosostris, with her bad cold, is an ironic version of the prophetic figure. Her name itself sounds like a cheap imitation of some Egyptian deity and the Tarot pack which, according to Jessie Weston, had played such a central part in the most crucial fertility rites of Ancient Egypt, has now become part of the equipment of a bogus fortune-teller. Nonetheless, the paradox of Madame Sosostris being 'the wisest woman in Europe,/With a wicked pack of cards', is continued in the fact that, however bogus she may appear to be or even try to be, her reading of the cards does foretell the events and characters of the poem. Little attempt is made by her to explain the cards and she offers only one piece of advice: 'Fear death by drowning' but, in an indirect way, she indicates the nature of the waste land with its 'crowds of people, walking round in a ring', she sees the temptation of Belladonna and she points to the lack of spiritual enlightenment in the absence of the Hanged Man.

The description of London in the final paragraph of Part I provides evidence for Madame Sosostris's cryptic vision. Eliot, using a composite of Baudelaire's Paris, Dante's Hell and, according to Ezra Pound, the London of William Blake (1757–1827), creates a horrifying picture of people locked in a mindless, life-destroying routine. In Canto III of his *Hell*, Dante, after describing the stream of souls condemned for their spiritual emptiness, isolates one figure whom he recognises as a Pope who has been guilty of the cowardice of refusing high office and thereby allowing a wicked Pope to misgovern the Church. The figure of Stetson seems to be given a similar character by Eliot. By referring to Mylae, as well as to Dante's medieval Hell and Baudelaire's 'swarming city' of the nineteenth century, Eliot is anxious to stress that the problem he sees is not one unique to London in 1922, but is endemic to mankind. At one level, the conversation in the streets of London is a piece of macabre, surrealistic comedy, but, at its deeper level, the episode recalls the title of Part I, 'The Burial of the Dead' and the fertility rites which are so crucial to the meaning of the whole poem. Stetson, the reader, must tend the buried corpse, whether that corpse be an effigy of the god, a human sacrifice, or what the Bible calls 'the old man' which the Christian has to bury before a new life is possible (see Romans, Chapter 6). Man's friend, the Dog, could be any temptation to man to look for easy solutions, short-cuts or the kind of apathy or indolence described in the opening lines of the poem.

NOTES AND GLOSSARY:

Title:	it comes from the burial service of the Anglican Church
tubers:	swollen roots providing nourishment for the future growth of a plant
Starnbergersee:	lake near Munich, in Bavaria, a fashionable resort visited by Eliot in 1911
colonnade:	a covered walk with columns, like an arcade
Hofgarten:	public park in Munich
Bin gar . . . deutsch:	(*German*) 'I am not Russian at all, I come from Lithuania, pure German'
the arch-duke's:	the arch-duke Ferdinand of Austria was assassinated in 1914 and his death was one of the immediate causes of the First World War
Marie:	Countess Marie Larisch who had many family connections with the royal families of Austria and Bavaria. Her book, *My Past*, describing these connections appeared in 1913. Eliot had already met her
Son of man:	the phrase used by God to address his prophet Ezekiel in the Old Testament of the Bible (Ezekiel 2:1). Ezekiel is commanded to preach against the wickedness of the Israelites
broken images:	God tells Ezekiel that he will break the idols (images) erected by the Israelites to false gods
the cricket no relief:	the sound of the grasshopper gives no comfort in the desert
There is . . . meet you:	these lines derive from the opening lines of Eliot's early poem, *The Death of Saint Narcissus*
red rock:	in the Bible the prophet Isaiah predicts that, in a new, righteous kingdom, 'a man shall be as an hiding place from the wind, and a covert from the tempest; as rivers of water in a dry place, as the shadow of a great rock in a weary land.' (Isaiah 32:2)
handful of dust:	in biblical terms man's body comes from the dust and returns to dust
Frisch . . . du:	(*German*) 'The wind blows fresh towards the homeland; my Irish child, where are you waiting?' The lines come from the beginning of Wagner's opera, *Tristan and Isolde*

hyacinths: flowers symbolic of resurrection because, according to the Greek legend, they had sprung up from the blood of the slain youth Hyacinthus

Oed' . . . das Meer: (*German*) 'Waste and empty is the sea.' The line comes from the final Act of Wagner's *Tristan and Isolde*

Madame Sosostris, famous clairvoyante: a fortune-teller whose name Eliot borrowed from a similar character in *Crome Yellow* (1921), a novel by Aldous Huxley (1894–1963). There was also a Madame Helena Blavatsky (1831–91) who was famous for her knowledge of magic

pack of cards: Eliot does not mean the ordinary pack of playing cards but the Tarot pack, consisting of seventy-eight illustrated cards and widely used in casting horoscopes. Jessie Weston claimed that the cards dated back to ancient Egyptian times when they were used in the prediction of the rising and falling of the river Nile. She also connected the symbolism of the designs on the cards with the Grail story. In his note, Eliot concedes that he was not familiar with the exact details of the pack and there is little point in looking for the particular cards of the Tarot

Phoenician Sailor: Phoenicia was the area on the Eastern Mediterranean coast now occupied by Lebanon and Syria. It was the location of the annual ceremonies to commemorate the death and resurrection of the god Thammuz, and was famous for its sailors and traders. See also comments on Part IV 'Death by Water'

(Those are pearls that were his eyes.): a line from Shakespeare's *The Tempest* (1.ii.398). It comes from a song sung by Ariel suggesting to Ferdinand that his father, King Alonso, has been transformed by drowning into 'something rich and strange'

man with the three staves: in his note, Eliot says that this figure is associated by him, 'quite arbitrarily, with the Fisher King himself.' Although the poet claims that the man with the three staves is an 'authentic member of the Tarot pack', it is difficult to see which card he had in mind

Belladonna . . . of situations: in Italian, 'belle donna' means beautiful lady. Belledonna is also the name of a poisonous flower used in cosmetics. Eliot may be referring in these lines to a description by Walter Pater (1839–94) of the famous painting of Mona Lisa by Leonardo da Vinci (1452–1519): 'She is older than the rocks among which she sits; like the vampire, she has been dead many times, and learned the secrets of the grave; and has been a diver in deep seas, and keeps their fallen day about her; and trafficked for strange webs with Eastern merchants'

the Wheel: the cycle of fortune

one-eyed merchant: anticipates Mr Eugenides in line 209. He is 'one-eyed' because he appears in profile on the card and because he is a man of limited vision

Which is blank . . . see: according to Jessie Weston, the traders from the Levant acted as carriers for religious beliefs and legends such as the story of the Grail but they themselves did not necessarily understand the significance of their stories. Madame Sosostris has no comprehension of these mysteries

Hanged Man: an actual figure in the Tarot pack. Eliot saw a connection between this figure and the Hanged God discussed by Frazer in *The Golden Bough* and he is associated by the poet with the hooded figure in line 363. The Hanged Man symbolises the sacrifice of one person or god to ensure the regeneration of fertility

thank you: she has been paid

Mrs Equitone: a client of the fortune-teller

horoscope: a plan of a person's character and prospects calculated by a study of the stars and planets prominent at the time of his birth

Unreal City: the City in London is the business centre of London and the place where Eliot worked at the time of writing *The Waste Land*. In his note, Eliot refers to lines in Baudelaire's poem, 'The Seven Old Men': 'Swarming city, city full of dreams, where the ghost, in broad daylight, stops the passer-by'

brown fog: the heavy fog mixed with the dirty smoke from factories

London Bridge: bridge across the River Thames leading to the City

I had not thought death had undone so many: Eliot takes the line from Dante's *Hell*, Canto III: 'such a long stream of people that I should never have believed that death had undone so many.' The people described had lived selfishly and had known neither good nor evil

Sighs, short and infrequent, were exhaled: Eliot draws our attention to lines in Dante's *Hell*, Canto IV: 'Here, so far as I could tell, there was no lamentation except sighs, which caused the eternal air to tremble.' The sighs are uttered by those who had lived good lives but without Christian knowledge. In limbo, this part of Hell, the souls have desire for God but lack hope

King William Street: in the City of London

Saint Mary Woolnoth: a church in the City dating back to the twelfth century but restored and rebuilt in the seventeenth and eighteenth centuries. A report in 1920 suggested that it should be demolished; Eliot with others opposed this move

dead sound on the final stroke of nine: the bell attached to the church clock does not strike properly on the ninth stroke. 9 am is the hour when offices in the City would open for work. According to the Gospel, Christ died at the ninth hour and Eliot may have had this echo in his mind

Mylae: a battle (260 BC) in the first Punic War between the Romans and the Carthaginians to determine who should control trade in the Mediterranean. The Carthaginians are related to the Phoenicians who appear elsewhere in the poem

That corpse . . . again: According to a myth in Ancient Egypt, the semi-divine Osiris was murdered by his rival Set and the torn pieces of his body were buried in different places in Egypt. His wife, Isis, usually associated with the Nile, made those graves into holy places and each year grain was planted above them. When the grain sprouted, the people recognised that Osiris was not really dead but was resurrected in the new crops. An effigy of Osiris was also floated on the currents across the eastern Mediterranean from Alexandria to Byblos to symbolise the dying and rebirth of the year. Sirius, the Dog Star, was associated with the annual flooding of the Nile

Stetson:	Eliot claimed that he had no particular person in mind but wished to suggest the typical businessman of the City. The word 'stetson', however, is the name of the large hat worn by cowboys and some people felt that Eliot must have been referring to Pound who wore such a hat. Eliot denied this
the Dog:	Eliot refers us to *The White Devil*, by John Webster (1580–1638), 5.IV where Cordelia is singing a lament for 'the friendless bodies of unburied men'. She goes on to say, 'But keep the wolf far hence, that's foe to men,/For with his nails he'll dig them up again.' Webster's 'wolf' is changed by Eliot to 'Dog' to fit the lines into the London street scene. The capital letter is Eliot's way of generalising the idea of the dog

'You hypocrite lecteur—mon semblable,—mon frere': (*French*) Eliot takes the line from the introductory poem, 'To the Reader,' in Baudelaire's *Flowers of Evil*. In the poem Baudelaire states that we are all guilty of 'stupidity, error, sin and meanness' but, worst of all, of boredom, spiritual emptiness, and he involves the reader in his disgust by addressing him finally as, 'Hypocrite reader, my fellow-man, my brother!'

II. A Game of Chess

In Middleton's *Women Beware Women*, each move in the game of chess is matched by a move in the seduction of Bianca. It is a story of lust, manipulation and deceit. In this part of *The Waste Land*, Eliot, while focusing on two modern episodes, incorporates a wide range of references to women who were victims of lust and deceit.

The first episode (down to line 138) is given an elaborate, mock-epic setting. The description of the room carries memories of the meeting of famous lovers like Antony and Cleopatra and Dido and Aeneas but the ornateness of the decorations has an excessive and artificial quality. The convoluted syntax of the long sentences leads the reader into confusion but, as the description moves to the picture of Philomel, a more sinister element disturbs the mind. Philomel was cruelly assaulted and given the voice of the nightingale to proclaim her wrong but the world (and the 'hypocrite reader') still relentlessly pursues her. The sickly oppressiveness of the room leads into the claustrophobic hysteria of the woman.

The inverted commas indicate the words of the woman, anxious and questioning. The lines in between the woman's questions belong to her male companion and the lack of inverted commas suggests that we are overhearing his thoughts and not his words. He seems resigned and even playful, though in a macabre way, as if he has heard her frantic questions so often before that he knows proper replies to be useless. His state of mind, however, does not suggest health but a preoccupation with loss and death.

The second episode, beginning at line 139, is set in a pub in the Cockney area of London. Eliot, in a note on the typescript, said that he did not wish to indicate the Cockney pronunciation by using odd spelling but something of the intonation and style of Cockney English is communicated by him. The story told about Lil and Albert is sordid and lacking in any suggestion of love. Child-bearing is presented as a squalid burden with the wife's health and appearance deteriorating and the husband unsympathetic and irresponsible. The characters are trapped in time and no human value is asserted to give them dignity. Eliot emphasises the pressure of time by his repetition of the barman's imperious call. The sad sweetness of Ophelia's farewell merges with the voices of those leaving the pub and acts partly as a contrast in its grave refinement and partly as a parallel in that Ophelia's story, like Lil's, is one of deceit and incomprehension.

Despite the obvious differences in setting, language and social class between the two episodes, they share certain qualities very central to Eliot's view of the waste land. Both present sterile relationships between men and women; in the first episode, the characters no longer even communicate: the woman voices nervous questions but the man remains silent and detached; in the second episode, Lil already looks 'antique' at the age of thirty-one and her main effort appears to be the prevention of further children. Behind the tawdry lives they live, where they seem like pawns in a game of chess rather than controllers, is the fear of decay and death, the cold 'wind under the door'.

NOTES AND GLOSSARY:

The title: a reference to the scene in the play *Women Beware Women* (1621) by Thomas Middleton (1580–1627), where Bianca is seduced by the Duke while her mother-in-law is diverted by a game of chess with the woman who has arranged the seduction. The original title, 'In the Cage', referred to the epigraph describing the fate of the Cumaean Sybil

glass: mirror

The Chair . . . throne: Eliot notes his debt to Shakespeare's *Antony and Cleopatra*, 2.ii. where Enobarbus describes Cleopatra's barge at her first meeting with Antony: 'The barge she sat in, like a burnished throne,/Burned on the water . . .' There are further echoes of Enobarbus's description in the following lines. 'Burnished' means polished

standards wrought with fruited vines: columns decorated with moulded grapes and vine leaves

Cupidon: a sculpted representation of the boy god of love

Doubled: (the mirror) reflected

candelabra: elaborate candlesticks

vials: small bottles

synthetic: mixed, blended, but with a strong suggestion of artificiality

unguent: ointment

laquearia: panelled ceiling. Eliot in his notes quotes from Book I of *Aeneid* by the Roman poet Virgil (70– 19 BC): 'flaming torches hang from the gold-panelled ceiling, and the torches conquer the night with flames.' The scene describes the banquet given by Dido, Queen of Carthage, in honour of Aeneas. He makes love to her but later deserts her

coffered: panelled

Huge sea-wood fed with copper: logs of drift-wood (from the sea) with copper in them are burning in the fire. The salt and copper burn with orange and green flames

dolphin: a symbol of love in medieval times

sylvan scene: the wooded area around the Garden of Eden as seen by Satan intent on seducing man from God in Milton's *Paradise Lost* (1667)

The change of Philomel . . . forced: Philomela was raped by her brother-in-law, King Tereus, and he cut out her tongue to prevent her from telling her sister. The gods transformed her into a nightingale. The story is told in the *Metamorphoses*, (changes of form) a Latin poem by Ovid (43 BC–AD 17)

inviolable: cannot be injured or profaned

'Jug Jug' to dirty ears: (a) the song of the nightingale (as represented in Elizabethan poetry); (b) 'jug' was also a form of vulgar sexual address. The same sound is heard differently by different listeners. See line 204

withered stumps of time: old legends but also a reference to Philomel's ripped tongue

staring forms: portraits, or figures in the paintings

rats' alley: Eliot connects this line with line 195

pearls: see note on page 22. Originally, Eliot's line read: 'The hyacinth garden. Those are pearls that were his eyes, yes!'

O O O O that Shakespeherean Rag: a rag is a piece of jazz dance music. Eliot's line comes from 'The Shakespeherean Rag', a popular song of 1912 and has the rhythm typical of ragtime music

game of chess: see note on title of this part. Originally, there was a line between the present lines 137 and 138 which read: 'The ivory men make company between us'

lidless: sleepless, uncomfortable

demobbed: short for 'demobilised', meaning released from the army back into civilian life

I didn't mince my words: I told her directly

Hurry up please it's time: the call of the barman at closing time in a British pub (a shortened form of public house, a place where alcoholic drinks can be bought and consumed during certain hours fixed by law), telling people to finish their drinks and leave

straight: challenging

you can get on with it: you will have to accept it

pulling a long face: adopting a dejected expression

to bring it off: to induce an abortion

gammon: smoked ham

ta ta: goodbye (*slang*)

Good night . . . good night: the line comes from Shakespeare's *Hamlet*, 5.iv. when Ophelia, driven mad by the death of her father and her confused love for Hamlet, bids farewell before going to drown herself

III. The Fire Sermon

Just as in Part I, the title 'The Burial of the Dead' does not explain itself till Stetson's planted corpse appears at the end, so the force of the title 'The Fire Sermon' is not made clear till Eliot invokes the Buddha and St Augustine in the final lines of Part III. In his notes on these lines, Eliot stresses the importance he attaches to the teaching of those saints of east and west, both of whom had experienced the pleasures of the body before deciding to follow a spiritual path. In this part of the poem, Eliot presents a series of incidents which demonstrate his agreement with the decision of the two ascetic figures.

The first section (lines 173–186) uses Spenser's idealised vision of human love in the setting of an earthly paradise where the nymphs of the pure river celebrate the wedding as a background contrast to the example of casual, sordid modern sex. Nature itself is now spoiled and the clutching fingers of leaves suggest a desperation. The recurring refrain from Spenser's joyful wedding poem now sounds plaintive or even mocking. What song can the poet sing in the brown land where the river is now polluted with the rubbish of uncaring people? This modern location is the land of captivity, of lamentation and always the poet is made aware of how dead the land and the people have become.

Joining the second section (lines 187–202) to the first are echoes from the scene in James Joyce's *Ulysses* when Bloom goes to the funeral of Paddy Dignam: 'the rattle of bones', the rat, the canal and the gasworks all evoke the unpleasant episode of the funeral. In the gloomy industrial setting with its canal and gasworks the speaker, who is linked to Prince Ferdinand in *The Tempest*, fishes on a winter evening. The death of his father and brother who were both king suggests that he is now king himself, the Fisher King of the waste land. There seems little hope of his catching a fish in a polluted canal in winter and his thoughts are fixed on the unburied remains of his relatives. Spring has not yet arrived but it does not promise any purification or fertility. The hectic traffic of the city and the sordid relationship of Sweeney and Mrs Porter are in sad contrast to the heroic hunt and the encounter between the Goddess of chastity and Actaeon. Similarly, the farcical washing of the prostitutes' feet is a parody of the feet-washing ceremony in the chapel of the grail celebrated by the choir of boys.

The little section (lines 203–206) with the nightingale's song reminds us of the story of Philomel described in lines 99–103 and emphasises the themes of assaulted innocence and the power of lust.

In the following lines (207–214), Eliot reinforces his general claim that London, representative of urban living, is corrupt and has lost its spiritual vision. The Smyrna merchant, one-eyed we remember, is a decadent version of the Phoenician traders who, according to Jessie Weston, had transmitted knowledge of the fertility religions in the old days. The merchant's appearance, his unimpressive samples, his crude language, his suspect invitation,—all indicate the fallen nature of the modern trader.

In 'The Fire Sermon' sexual relations are presented as violent or mechanical; respect and affection are absent. In the episode of the typist and the 'young man carbuncular', Eliot's concern is to show their mechanical behaviour. He opens the description by suggesting an automatic quality in the eyes and back of the office worker who is reduced in the monotony of his work to the status of a 'human engine'. The typist's life seems to be contained in the display of her clothes and food; she is bored and tired, has nothing to offer or withhold. The clerk accomplishes his sexual task without apparent pleasure and the actions do not affect either character. Do they have personalities which can be affected? The casual but obvious rhymes make each action predictable and dispassionate and nowhere is this more striking than in the final four lines (253-256) where the typist's easy acceptance of her dishonour is in contrast to the anguished song of Olivia in Goldsmith's novel.

The role of Tiresias in the poem is indicated in Eliot's note on line 218 and in this section he provides a crucial time dimension to the episode. In the particularities of his description and by involving contrasting examples from earlier periods (for example, Sappho and Goldsmith), Eliot seems to attribute a unique squalor to the modern world; Tiresias, however, assures us that he, with his comprehensive experience of the living and the dead, has seen all this before.

Line 257, 'This music crept by me upon the waters' refers backwards to the previous record on the gramophone, back also to Ferdinand in lines 191-192, and forward to 'the pleasant whining of a mandoline' (line 261). The line works differently with each of these references: the record with which the woman anaesthetises her feelings pervades the city and is a cold reminder of human insensitivity; the music Ferdinand heard was Ariel's song of consolation to him and this music might counteract the nastiness of the previous scene; the mandoline is a 'pleasant whining', a paradoxical description which combines pleasure and pain. This section (lines 257-265) certainly offers a pleasing sensation but there are hints that the sensation is flimsy and not to be trusted too far. The poet's, 'O City city,' has a distinctly solemn tone, the lounging fishmen are not fishermen and the glory of the church is a physical one and not necessarily spiritual.

For those readers who know Wagner's operas, it is easy to see a connection between the 'splendour of . . . white and gold' (line 265) and the shining of the sacred gold in the river, the loss of which is lamented by the Rhine-maidens in the passage down to line 306. The opening description of the Thames is reminiscent of the description of the same river at the beginning of Conrad's *Heart of Darkness*, a book greatly admired by Eliot, in which Conrad tries to show how precarious our civilisation is and how depraved the human heart can be. The modern and the renaissance Thames with its traffic has an obvious appeal but the lament of the Rhine-maidens reminds us that something has been lost. Even the spectacle of Queen Elizabeth in a golden barge like Cleopatra's, the sound of bells on the wind and the white towers cannot balance the lament. The three river-maidens tell the same story of violation and confusion; they appear to have no hope or impetus towards a new life. In the three accounts (lines 292–305) by the Thames-girls there is a progression in degradation as if the three reports could be by the same person describing her fall from honour, the situation 'after the event' and her descent into a state of madness where her world has fallen apart and even her command of language has broken down.

The final lines (307–311) of Part III do offer some hope in that the Buddha and St Augustine each came to an understanding of his problem and saw a way forward. St Augustine's expression of gratitude is the only explicit invocation of God in the entire poem. The spacing of these lines, however, with the final burning left trailing without a full stop, may suggest that there is no one final solution to the problem of human sin, or at least that it is not clear at this point in the poem.

NOTES AND GLOSSARY:

The title: In his note to line 308, Eliot refers his reader to the Buddha's Fire Sermon (fifth century BC). The Buddha tells his followers that the human senses and all that they perceive are burning: 'With what fire are they burning? I declare to you that they are burning with the fire of lust, with the fire of anger, with the fire of ignorance, with the concerns of birth, decay, death, grief, lamentation, misery, dejection and despair.' The follower who studies the scriptures and follows the Noble Path, becomes weary of the things of the senses and rids himself of all passion and so becomes free of the cycle of birth and death and rebirth. In Christianity, fire is a common symbol of lust and also of the purifying power of God

river's tent: the leaves on the trees form an arch over the river

nymphs: beautiful young girls in classical legend

Sweet Thames, runs softly, till I end my song: the line comes from the refrain of *Prothalamion* by Edmund Spenser (1552–1599). The poem celebrates an aristocratic wedding on the banks of the River Thames in beautiful surroundings in summer

testimony: evidence

addresses: addresses to which mail can be forwarded or at which the men can be found and made to fulfil their responsibilities to the girls

waters of Leman: In the Bible, the Hebrews recall their exile in Babylon and how they longed for their homeland: 'By the rivers of Babylon, there we sat down, yea, we wept, when we remembered Zion . . . How shall we sing the lord's song in a strange land?' (Psalm 137). Lake Leman is the French name for Lake Geneva in Switzerland near where Eliot received treatment for his mental illness in 1921 while he was writing part of *The Waste Land*. The archaic word 'leman' means a mistress

But at my back . . . to ear: Eliot's lines recall lines from 'To His Coy Mistress' by Andrew Marvell (1621–1678): 'But at my back I always hear/Time's winged chariot hurrying near.' The poet urges the girl to make love with him because time and eventually death are pressing in on them

gashouse: American word for gasworks

Musing . . . before him: Eliot refers the reader to Shakespeare's *The Tempest*: 'Sitting on a bank,/Weeping again the King my father's wreck,/This music crept by me upon the waters,/Allaying both their fury and my passion/With its sweet air' (1.ii.389–92). Ferdinand is lamenting his father's death and is comforted by Ariel's music. See also lines 48 and 257

garret: a small room in the attic

But . . . hear: see note above on 'But at my back . . .'

But . . . in the spring: Eliot refers the reader to lines in *The Parliament of Bees*, a play by John Day (1574–1640): 'When of the sudden, listening, you shall hear,/A noise of horns and hunting, which shall bring/Actaeon to Diana in the spring,/Where all shall see her naked skin . . .' Actaeon was out hunting, according to the Greek legend, when he came on Diana, the goddess of chastity, bathing with her nymphs. As a punishment for his lack of self-control he was changed into a stag and hunted to death by his own hounds.

                      Sweeney is a character who represents brutish vigour and sexual vulgarity. Mrs Porter is a woman of doubtful virtue (see following note)

O the moon . . . water: Eliot took these lines from a polite version of a vulgar ballad popular among Australian soldiers in the First World War. Mrs Porter may have been a famous brothel-keeper. The moon was special to the goddess Diana and a symbol of her purity. The 'soda water' is a cleaning solution not a drink

Et O ces voix d'enfants, chantant dans la coupole: (*French*) 'And, O those children's voices singing in the dome.' The line comes from 'Parsifal' by Paul Verlaine (1844–1896). The poem, following Wagner's opera, describes how the questing hero Parsifal has withstood all temptations and succeeded in curing the wounded king, Amfortas (the Fisher King). Parsifal's feet are washed and the choir of boys in the chapel of the Holy Grail sing a song of celebration

Twit . . . Tereu: the song of the raped Philomel transformed into a nightingale harks back to lines 99–103. Eliot also borrows from a song by John Lyly (1554–1606): 'What bird so sings, yet so does wail?/Oh, 'tis the ravished nightingale,/Jug, jug, jug, jug, tereu, she cries,/And still her woes at midnight rise.' 'Twit' is a common imitation of bird song; 'tereu' means 'O, Tereus' (the king who raped Philomel)

Mr Eugenides, the Smyrna merchant: Smyrna is the old name for Izmir, a seaport in western Turkey, and it can be connected with Phoenician places and people elsewhere in the poem. The name 'Mr Eugenides' means 'well-born' but, like 'Mrs Equitone' (line 57), it sounds artificial. Eliot, in his notes, connects this merchant with 'the one-eyed merchant' (line 52) and with the Phoenecian sailor (line 47) who appears as Phlebas in Part IV

C.i.f. London: documents at sight: Eliot explains that the price of the merchant's currants includes 'cost, insurance and freight to London' and that the ownership papers for the currants would be given to the buyer in London on receipt of a bank draft

demotic: vulgar, uneducated

Cannon Street Hotel: an hotel beside a railway station in the City of London. This station served the routes to Continental Europe and the hotel was, consequently, popular with travelling businessmen

the Metropole: fashionable hotel in Brighton, on the south coast of England, about one hour's journey from London. A 'weekend in Brighton' can suggest an illicit sexual meeting

violet hour: dusk when the sky can be a purplish-blue colour. The flower, the violet, was, perhaps because of its use in perfumes, associated through classical and medieval times with sex

human engine: worker

I Tiresias . . . can see: Eliot's note reads: 'Tiresias, although a mere spectator and not indeed a "character," is yet the most important personage in the poem, uniting all the rest. Just as the one-eyed merchant, seller of currants, melts into the Phoenician Sailor, and the latter is not wholly distinct from Ferdinand Prince of Naples, so all the women are one woman, and the two sexes meet in Tiresias. What Tiresias SEES, in fact, is the substance of the poem.'

He then quotes the story of Tiresias from *Metamorphoses* by Ovid: 'Jupiter jokingly said to Juno, "You women receive much more pleasure in love than men do." Juno denied the claim. They decided to ask the wise Tiresias for his opinion because he knew love from both sides. Once, when two huge snakes were copulating in the green forest, he had struck them with his stick; he was miraculously transformed into a woman and lived as a female for seven years. In the eighth year he again saw the snakes and said: "If a blow of my stick had the magic to change my sex, I shall now strike you again." He struck the snakes, and he was restored to his original sex. For this reason he was asked to judge the Gods' playful argument; he supported Jupiter. Juno, it is claimed, was needlessly angered and she condemned the judge, Tiresias, to everlasting blindness. It is not permitted for one god to reverse the act of another god, but the all powerful father, to recompense Tiresias for the loss of his sight, gave him the power to know the future and so honoured Tiresias.'

Tiresias was the most famous prophet of the classical world

At the . . . sea: Eliot had in mind the coastal fishermen who return to port at dusk. He refers us to lines by Sappho, the sixth century BC Greek poetess: 'Thou, evening star, who draws homeward all that the radiant dawn sent out . . .' There is an echo of the end of 'Requiem' by R.L. Stevenson (1850–1894): 'Home is the sailor, home from sea,/And the hunter home from the hill'

combinations: under-garments

camisoles, and stays: under-garments and corsets (artificial support for her figure)

old man with wrinkled dugs: Tiresias has shrivelled female breasts as part of his bi-sexuality (see note above on 'I Tiresias . . .')

carbuncular: with pimples

One . . . millionaire: Bradford is a town in the north of England which manufactures woollen goods. Many manufacturers made large profits during the First World War and the lines suggest the vulgarity of newly acquired wealth. The north of England is often considered vulgar and unsophisticated by cultured Londoners and Eliot is sharing that prejudice

propitious: suitable, favourable

foresuffered: experienced; one who has felt pain before

I who . . . wall: in *King Oedipus* by Sophocles (495–406 BC) the prophet Tiresias knows that the city of Thebes is suffering sterility and plague because Oedipus has unknowingly killed his father and married his own mother and the gods have cursed the city

And walked . . . dead: in *The Odyssey* by Homer (about eighth century BC) when Odysseus visits Hades (the Greek underworld of the dead), he is advised by Tiresias who, though dead, still sees the future of the living

patronising: as if he thinks he is doing her an honour

When . . . the gramophone: Eliot refers his reader to the novel, *The Vicar of Wakefield* by Oliver Goldsmith (1730–1774). Olivia who has been seduced sings: 'When lovely woman stoops to folly,/And finds too late that men betray,/What charm can soothe her melancholy?/What art can wash her guilt away?/The only art her guilt to cover,/To hide her shame from every eye,/To give repentence to her lover,/And wring his bosom, is—to die'

'This music . . . waters': see note on page 32 on 'Musing . . . before him'

the Strand: one of the main streets in London, joining Westminster to the City. Formerly, its big houses backed onto the River Thames

Queen Victoria Street: in the City and close to the Thames

O City city: possibly an allusion to the cry of Jesus against the blindness of the city of Jerusalem of his time: 'O Jerusalem, Jerusalem, thou that killest the prophets, and stonest them that are sent unto thee, how often would I have gathered thy children together, even as a hen gathereth her chickens under her wings, and ye would not! Behold, your house is left unto you desolate' (Matthew,23)

lower Thames Street: in the City on the Thames

mandoline: a stringed musical instrument

fishmen: workers from the nearby Billingsgate fishmarket

Magnus Martyr: the church of St Magnus Martyr, near London Bridge and the fishmarket, was rebuilt in the seventeenth century after the Great Fire of London had destroyed it. Its interior was designed by the architect Sir Christopher Wren (1632–1723). Eliot campaigned for its restoration

inexplicable: cannot be explained

Ionian: one of the three styles of Grecian architecture. In the original manuscript Eliot described the style as 'Corinthian'. Although these names have a strictly technical sense, it is possibly significant that both 'Ionian' and 'Corinthian' can be used to mean decadent

The river . . . la la: Eliot points out that 'the Song of the (three) Thames-daughters begins here. From line 292 to 306 inclusive they speak in turn.' He compares his Thames-daughters with the Rhine-maidens in Wagner's opera, *The Twilight of the Gods*. The Rhine-maidens lament the sacred gold which has been stolen from the River Rhine and the theft has brought a dullness to the river. At the end of the story the gold in the shape of a ring is recovered by the maidens from a huge fire in which the bodies of the hero and heroine have been burned

sweats: the oil and tar in the river come to the surface and float like sweat on skin

wash: the wave caused by the boat's movement

Greenwich reach: stretch of the Thames downstream from the centre of London

Isle of Dogs: the bank of the river opposite Greenwich, part of London's dock area

Weialala . . . leialala: the chorus from the Rhine-maidens' lament (see note on 'The river . . .' above)

Elizabeth and Leicester: Queen Elizabeth I of England and Lord Robert Dudley, the Earl of Leicester, one of the Queen's favourites. Eliot refers the reader to a letter written in 1561 by the Spanish Ambassador to his master King Philip of Spain in which he describes Elizabeth and Leicester: 'In the afternoon we were in a barge, watching the games on the river. She was alone with the Lord Robert and myself on the poop, when they began to talk nonsense and went so far that Lord Robert at last said, as I was on the spot [he was a bishop] there was no reason why they should not be married if the Queen pleased.' Elizabeth never got married, had no children and was proud of her title, the Virgin Queen

Highbury . . . Undid me: Eliot imitates words from Dante's *Purgatory*: 'Remember me, who am La Pia (Piety); Siena made me, Maremma undid me.' Siena and Maremma are places in Tuscany in Italy and La Pia was murdered by her husband. She is in Purgatory because she died before she had repented her life. Highbury is a residential area of London; Richmond and Kew are popular places to go to on boating trips

Supine: lying on her back

Moorgate: poorer area in the City

Margate Sands: a seaside resort on the Thames estuary, popular for day-trips from London. Eliot began *The Waste Land* in Margate when he was ill in October 1921

la la: the fading echo of the Rhine-maidens' lament

To Carthage then I came: Eliot takes the line from the *Confessions* of St Augustine (354–430): 'To Carthage then I came, where a cauldron of unholy loves sang all about my ears.' St Augustine, born in what is now Algeria, went to Carthage when he was sixteen and experienced the power of lust before he gradually discovered the value of spiritual love

Burning burning burning burning: see note on the title, 'The Fire Sermon'

O Lord . . . out: Eliot refers the reader to St Augustine's *Confessions*: 'I entangle my steps with these outward beauties, but Thou pluckest me out, O Lord, Thou pluckest me out.' In the Bible (Zechariah 3.2.), God rescues the corrupt high-priest from his sin and asks Satan, 'Is this not a brand plucked out of the fire?' Eliot comments that, 'The collocation of these two representatives (Buddha and St Augustine) of eastern and western asceticism, as the culmination of this part of the poem, is not an accident.'

IV. Death by Water

The original manuscript of Part IV had ninety-three lines and the deleted sections do help us to a fuller understanding of the surviving ten lines. A dead sailor, resembling Coleridge's Ancient Mariner, recounts the story of a fishing trip which ended in disaster. The story has close links with the final voyage of the Greek hero Odysseus (Ulysses) as imagined by Dante (*Hell*, xxvi) and Tennyson. Ulysses was seen by Dante and Tennyson as a man with an insatiable curiosity, unable to accept the idea of his dying, and driven to seek new experiences. His attitude is the extreme opposite of that of the Buddha and St Augustine expressed at the end of Part III. Furthermore, the surviving lines about Phlebas are virtually a translation of the final part of Eliot's poem, 'In the Restaurant', written in French some four years earlier. In that poem a dirty old waiter tells a customer how, at the age of seven, he had been on the point of having sex with a young girl when he was interrupted by the arrival of a big dog and he ran away. The following lines about Phlebas come after the waiter's sordid story: 'Phlebas the Phoenician, a fortnight drowned, forgot the cries of gulls and the swell of the Cornish seas and the profit and the loss, and the cargo of tin. An undersea current carried him very far, taking him back through the stages of his former life. Just imagine, it was a hard fate, considering he was once a tall, handsome man.' The implication is that Phlebas, like the waiter, had sought physical pleasure and not spiritual wisdom.

The waiter's story also helps to connect Phlebas with Mr Eugenides more securely. St Paul who was specially concerned with preaching the gospel to the Gentiles, wrote to his fellow missionary, Timothy: 'But they that will be rich fall into temptation and a snare, and into many foolish and hurtful lusts, which drown men in destruction and perdition' (1 Timothy 6:9). The merchant is trapped in his ambitions. Eliot, so fascinated by Conrad's account of Kurtz's degeneration in *The Heart of Darkness*, must have remembered the story-teller's question: 'Did he live his life again in every detail of desire, temptation, and surrender during that supreme moment of complete knowledge? He cried in a whisper at some image, at some vision—he cried out twice, a cry that was no more than a breath—"The horror! The horror!"' Phlebas has passed beyond such urgency but, in entering the whirlpool, he is locked in the cycle of his futile life, his death is fruitless. Jessie Weston, in her book, discusses how a wooden effigy of the god of fertility was thrown into the sea at Alexandria and carried by the current to the Phoenician coast, a symbol of the dying and rebirth of the year, a fruitful death by water. Eliot warns the reader to learn from the sad example of Phlebas and give careful thought to the direction of his life.

NOTES AND GLOSSARY:

The title: an apparent contrast to 'The Fire Sermon' and burning of Part III. Compare also lines 47 and 55

Phlebas the Phoenician: according to Eliot's note on line 218 he is a further aspect of the one-eyed merchant Mr Eugenides

current: the flow of water may be a mocking pun on his pocket full of dried grapes (compare line 210)

Gentile or Jew: a Gentile is any non-Jewish person. In the New Testament the two are taken to include all mankind and both are equally welcome to the gift of Christianity

wheel: steering wheel of a boat; also the wheel of fortune (compare line 51)

windward: the direction from which the wind is blowing

V. What the Thunder Said

The first fifty lines of Part V are set in the bleak desert landscape visited briefly in Part I and the longed for rain is not seen to arrive throughout Part V. There is an atmosphere of remembered drama lapsing into anticlimax in lines 322–330. After the momentous and painful last hours of Jesus's life, the man whom his followers had believed was a god is dead. In lines reminiscent of the words of the inhabitants of the dead land (lines 1–7), they accept a minimal life without obvious hope of a resurrection; only the distant rolling of thunder beyond the mountains suggests spring and a new start.

In the second paragraph (lines 331–358), Eliot describes the journey through the waste land. The questing knight in his search for the Grail has to travel through inhospitable territory where he is subject to horrifying delusions. Hope on this journey in the desert is merely hypothetical: the form of the paragraph is determined by a series of 'ifs' with their answering 'buts'. The desert takes on a malevolent appearance, taunting and frightening the traveller. Water, the source of life, is totally absent. In the first paragraph the controlling word is 'after'; now, after the death of the god, the wounding of the Fisher King, the loss of personal faith, man must confront his own impotence.

Paragraphs three and four (lines 359–376) can be taken together. Eliot indicates in his notes that he is describing the journey to Emmaus and the decay of eastern Europe centred on the Communist Revolution in Russia. The disciples of Jesus, stunned by his death, are so blinded by their own helplessness that when the resurrected Jesus appears they fail to recognise him. Reality and hallucination cannot be distinguished by them. In his final message to his followers, Jesus warned of cruel times to come when there would be oppression and false prophets. For Eliot, Russian Communism with its atheist creed offered deluding prophecies to the blinded masses and now they stumble about in their spiritual desert. Russia, however, is not unique but merely one aspect of the cycle of error and destruction seen throughout history. All men share the tendency to accept the unreal world as if it were the real. Eliot here suggests the contrast, specifically described by St Augustine, between the City of Destruction with its false values and the City of God with its Christian values.

Both the journey to Emmaus and the swarming over plains are examples of misguided pilgrimages but enlightenment can take place in unlikely circumstances. These two journeys are aspects of the knight's journey in search of the Grail. In the following two paragraphs (lines 377–394) the horrifying details of the knight's journey are described. Many of these details remind us of times which have occurred earlier in the poem; just as the five questions in lines 359–371 echo the anxious questions of the woman in Part II, her room is recalled and turned upside down in lines 377–381. The knight's ordinary power of perception is upset and he is mocked by echoes and hallucinations. His mind is on the edge of madness and the ruined chapel in its desolate location in the deceptive moonlight seems like a cruel joke after the agonies of his journey. The omens are not promising but the appearance of the cock heralds a new dawn and the flash of lightning intimates the arrival of the long awaited rain. In the knight's acceptance of his own emptiness, a miracle can take place.

The thunder section (lines 395–422) seems to happen parallel to the climax of the quest for the Holy Grail and even takes the place of the expected questions to the Grail. The country of India is still in the dry season and nature awaits the coming of the rain. In this case, however, the thunder announces not rain but the advice by which men's lives can be revitalised. As at the end of Part III where St Augustine and the Buddha are united, Eliot is intent here on joining western and eastern wisdoms together. Eliot may also be making a criticism of the state of the Christian church in Europe and suggesting that western man has to look outside his over-familiar systems to find fresh inspiration in the east; this reading of Eliot's intention squares with the gloomy thought in lines 410-416. Eliot chooses to go back to an older wisdom whose very language lies behind all the varied developments of the Indo-European peoples. The words of advice (give, sympathise, control) heard in the sound of the thunder are straightforward and are central to the major religions. In the waste land, these virtues are absent.

Eliot presents three confessions illustrating the mentality of the waste land in an attempt to diagnose the spiritual emptiness which results from ignoring the teaching of the thunder. In the first, it is difficult to determine to whom it is addressed; 'my friend' was originally 'my brother' and it seems likely that the reader is being confided in. It is possible also that, if the surrender is sexual, the 'I' could be female and, indeed, the encounter described has a similarity to Francesca's account to Dante of her fateful love for Paulo (*Hell*, V). This account, however, has little in common with the various surrenders in Part III, 'The Fire Sermon': the speaker here is trembling with emotion and the surrender is a supreme moment, a moment of giving. There is, nonetheless, an undoubted suggestion of folly which 'an age of prudence can never retract'. Such is the general dullness of the person's life that this moment is unique but secret and it does not appear in the public or official accounts of his life. Mention of empty rooms, obituaries and the solicitor suggests that he considers himself already dead but there are parallels between this experience and the relationship with the hyacinth girl in Part I.

In answer to the challenge to sympathise or show compassion, the speaker confesses that, from his point of view, each individual is separated from all others and such is the self-centredness of people that they live locked away from each other. Both Count Ugolino and Coriolanus were led by their self-seeking nature into treachery against their own people and, because they can show no sympathy for others, they bring on themselves cruel punishment. The woman in the room in 'A Game of Chess' is similarly imprisoned in her own anxious mentality.

The third aspect of giving, according to the thunder, is control and, in particular, self restraint. The connection between giving and control is not immediately obvious but Eliot's example does help to explain the connection. Without self-control one cannot give to another. If Coriolanus, for example, had learned to restrain his arrogance he could have communicated with his fellow Romans but he was so concerned with his image of himself, 'the key', that he could not appreciate the situation around him. Eliot uses the analogy of sailing to explore what can take place between two people. The good sailor does not impose rigid control on his boat; he accepts the power of wind and water and bases his steering of the boat on his understanding of this power. The boat 'responded gaily' as if glad to co-operate with man and wind and sea. Unfortunately, there are few other examples of this co-operative activity between man and nature elsewhere in the poem. Too often, as in both the episodes in Part II, the opposite happens and people choose to live artificially. The speaker in line 420 says, 'Your heart would have responded' as the boat had but this verb is conditional and he cannot offer the right control, the appropriate invitation. He cannot do so because he has no self-control. Lines 279–289 offer a comparable situation where Elizabeth and Leicester have the chance to develop a relationship of mutuality but, instead, they turn the situation into a silly game and so remain trapped in their own solitudes.

The three virtues advocated by the thunder are not to be separated from each other; they depend on each other and, in a sense, are interchangeable. They are reasserted in the second last line of the poem, but before that line Eliot introduces some difficult fragments. The Fisher King, the quester, has crossed the waste land and reached the open sea. The chapel has been reached and the thunder has told how health can be restored to the people. In his question: 'Shall I at least set my lands in order?' there is a movement towards some positive action but there also appears to be a concession on his part that whatever he can do is very limited. The quotations which follow (lines 426–429) do not resolve our difficulty in understanding what he means. The line from the nursery rhyme and the line from de Nerval's poem 'The Disinherited' suggest that he is surrounded by ruins; the lines from Dante and *The Vigil of Venus* look forward to the possibility of new life. As if he sees the reader's difficulty, the king tells us that he has to take comfort where he can find it and it is fragmentary. His appeal to the swallow in line 428 is equally ambivalent. The reader by now knows the tragic story of Philomel and Procne and how they continue, as birds, to lament their fate. The swallow of Tennyson's poem carries a message of love and traditionally in England the swallows flying from the south announce the coming of summer; the bird is a good omen and, according to a legend, it flew over the crucified Jesus singing, 'Console'.

This apparent confusion is probably deliberate. Throughout the poem, Eliot has used many techniques to widen the scope and application of his vision of life. At the end of each part, the reader feels himself addressed and the 'hypocrite reader' is caught again at the end of the poem. Hieronymo, driven partly mad by the cruelty and deceit around him, turns on the reader who thinks that the Fisher King is the man with the problem. Eliot forces the problems of the waste land on us because we, whether we know it or not, are the citizens of the 'unreal city' and we must find our Grail. The thunder repeats its advice and the mocking voice of Hieronymo is softened by the benediction of the last line.

NOTES AND GLOSSARY:

The title: In the Bible, God is often described as speaking to men with a voice of thunder. Thunder commonly intimates the arrival of rain. Eliot refers specifically to the message of the thunder given in Brihadaran-yaka-Upanishad one of the books in Sanskrit sacred to Hinduism (see note on page 45: 'Then spoke . . .')

torchlight . . . faces: a band of men came at night to arrest Jesus when he was betrayed by Judas

frosty . . . places: in the garden called Gethsemane Jesus prayed but his disciples could not keep awake. In St Luke's account, Jesus, 'Being in an agony . . . prayed more earnestly: and his sweat was as it were great drops of blood falling down to the ground'

prison and palace: the arrest of Jesus and his preliminary trial in the palace of the High Priest of the Jews before he was taken before Pilate, the Roman Governor in Jerusalem

reverberation/Of thunder: according to the account in the Bible, at the death of Jesus the earth shook and a sudden darkness took place. As well as the re-echoing of the thunder Eliot may have used 'reverberation' in its older sense of painful beating to refer to the beating inflicted on Jesus

carious: decayed, rotten

cicada: grasshopper characterised by its dry chirping noise (compare line 23) and related to the locust which eats all green growth and makes cultivated land into a desert

If there were water: (this does not count as a separate line but is numbered with 'And no rock')

hermit-thrush . . . drop: a shy North American bird celebrated, according to Eliot, for its 'water-dripping song'

Who . . . side of you?: Eliot refers the reader to Sir Ernest Shackleton's (1874–1922) account of his expedition in the Antarctic in which he describes how 'the party of explorers, at the extremity of their strength, had the constant delusion that there was one more member than could actually be counted.' Eliot also had in mind the account by St Luke of two disciples journeying on the road from Jerusalem to Emmaus after the death of their master, Jesus: 'And it came to pass, that, while they communed together and reasoned, Jesus himself drew near, and went with them. But their eyes were holden that they should not know him' (Luke 24:15–16)

lines 366–376: in his note, Eliot quotes a passage from *Glimpse into Chaos* (1920) by Herman Hesse (1877–1962): 'Already half of Europe, already at least half of Eastern Europe, on the way to chaos, drives drunkenly in spiritual frenzy along the edge of the abyss, and sings drunkenly, as though singing hymns, as Dmitri Karamazov [in *The Brothers Karamazov* by Fyodor Dostoevsky (1821–81)] sang. The offended bourgeois laughs at the songs; the saint and the seer hear them with tears.' Hesse was writing particularly about the Russian Revolution of 1917

Murmur of maternal lamentation: Eliot may be referring to St Luke's account of the crucifying of Jesus in which he writes: 'And there followed him a great company of people, and of women, which also bewailed and lamented him. But Jesus turning into them said, "Daughters of Jerusalem, weep not for me, but weep for yourselves, and for your children"' (Luke 23:27–28)

hooded: blindfolded

reforms: takes a new shape

Jerusalem . . . London: centres of civilisations

fiddled: played as if on a violin

reminiscent: prompting memories

bats . . . wells: the movement of Surrealism, fashionable in 1922, presented ordinary things in an extraordinary way so as to show them as comic or horrific. Eliot acknowledged a debt to Hieronymus Bosch (1460–1516) one of the models for the Surrealists of the twentieth century and whose paintings of Hell have details similar to those in Eliot's lines. In medieval versions of the quest for the Grail, the quester has to pass through temptations and horrors to prove his courage and faith

empty . . . wells: in the Bible God tells his prophet Jeremiah: 'My people have committed two evils; they have forsaken me, the fountain of living waters, and carved themselves out cisterns, broken cisterns that can hold no water' (Jeremiah 2:13)

tumbled . . . empty chapel: there is nothing in the Perilous Chapel and Perilous Cemetery to offer promise or hope to the quester. His last temptation is despair

cock: the cockerel announces the coming of daybreak and so, traditionally, it banishes ghosts and the powers of darkness. In Christian terms the cock crowing is firmly associated with Peter's denial of Jesus at the time of his trial in the palace of the High Priest. In his original manuscript Eliot has a 'black cock', commonly sacrificed in rituals to remove bad spirits

rooftree: the main beam supporting the ridge of the roof of the ruined chapel

Ganga: Ganges, the sacred river of India

Then spoke . . . Da: Eliot takes the story of the thunder from the Brihadaranyaka-Upanishad, one of India's holy books. Prajapati, the Creator, has three groups of offspring: gods, men and demons; they each seek his wisdom. To each he utters the syllable, 'Da', and asks if they understand. The gods think that he says, 'Restrain yourselves (damyata)', and he agrees. The men think that he says, 'Give (datta)', and he agrees. The demons think that he says 'Be compassionate (dayadhvam)', and he agrees. 'This same thing does the divine voice, thunder, repeat: "Da! Da! Da! that is, restrain yourselves, give, be compassionate."' 'Da' is the Sanskrit root of words relating to 'give'; it is also an imitation of the sound of thunder

Himavant:	holy mountain in the Himalayas between India and Tibet
Datta:	give
age:	old age or later years of life
retract:	withdraw, wipe out
obituaries:	brief biographies of the recently dead
memories . . . spider:	Eliot refers the reader to lines from *The White Devil* by John Webster: 'O men/That lie upon your death-beds, and are haunted/With howling wives, ne'er trust them, they'll remarry/Ere the worm pierce your winding-sheet: ere the spider/Make a thin curtain for your epitaphs. The characters in the play are strikingly passionate and deceitful. 'Beneficent' means kind or generous
under seals:	locked away and not to be opened before the person's death
Dayadhvam:	be compassionate, sympathise
I have . . . only:	Eliot refers to the story of Count Ugolino related in Dante's *Hell* (XXXIII). Ugolino, because of his political treachery, was locked up with his four sons in a tower and eventually they all died of hunger, the father being the last to die. He says, 'I heard below the door of the horrible tower nailed up . . . I did not weep, I so turned to stone inside.' In Hell he is dedicated to utter hatred against the man who had locked him in his prison
We think . . . the key:	in his note Eliot quotes from F. H. Bradley's *Appearance and Reality* (1893): 'My external sensations are no less private to my self than are my thoughts or my feelings. In either case my experience falls within my own circle, a circle closed on the outside; and, with all its elements alike, every sphere is opaque to the others which surround it . . . In brief, regarded as an existence which appears in a soul, the whole world for each is peculiar and private to that soul'
broken Coriolanus:	central character in Shakespeare's *Coriolanus*, he was brought up to despise the feelings of other people. His overwhelming pride and arrogance forced him into exile to fight with his previous enemies against his native Rome. The desperate appeal of his mother finally broke his self-confidence

aethereal rumours: vague, overheard comments by others or, more probably, his own insubstantial dreams

Damyata: control

I . . . fishing: the Fisher King has crossed his waste land and arrived at the sea

arid: the land is still barren

Shall . . . order?: in the Book of Isaiah, the land of Israel is described as made waste by the Assyrian invaders and 'In those days was King Hezekiah sick unto death. And Isaiah the prophet . . . came unto him, and said unto him, "Thus saith the Lord, Set thine house in order; for thou shalt die, and not live"' (Isaiah 38:1). Hezekiah prays for mercy and is granted fifteen extra years of life and the promise that the land will prosper

London Bridge . . . down: the line comes from a children's rhyme which probably had its origin in the ritual of human sacrifice in blessing new buildings

Poi . . . affina: Eliot takes the line from a passage in Dante's *Purgatory* (XXVI) where the Provençal poet Arnaut Daniel, condemned to burn for his lust during life, asks for Dante's sympathy: '"And so I pray you, by that virtue which guides you to the top of the stair, remember later on my pain." Then he hid himself in the fire which refines them.' Elsewhere Eliot speaks of the hope given by chosen suffering

Quando . . . chelidon: 'When shall I be like the swallow?' The line comes from an anonymous late Latin poem, *The Vigil of Venus*, which celebrates the arrival of spring and Venus, the goddess of love. The poem concludes with a passage about the raped Philomel (see note on page 27 who, in this account, was transformed into a swallow and her sister, Procne, into a nightingale. She asks when the spring will come for her, when she will become like the swallow and be able to sing. The refrain of the poem promises love to all

O swallow swallow: Eliot could be referring to a simple but misunderstood love song in 'The Princess' by Tennyson beginning, 'O swallow, swallow,' or to Algernon Swinburne's (1837–1909) poem 'Itylus' (Philomel) beginning, 'Swallow, my sister, O sister swallow,/ How can thine heart be full of the spring?'

Le Prince . . . abolie: (*French*) 'The Prince of Aquitaine in the ruined tower.' The line comes from the poem 'The Disinherited' by Gérard de Nerval (1808–1855); de Nerval suffered from fits of madness and felt an acute loneliness. One of the cards in the Tarot pack shows a tower struck by lightning and a Dark Tower occurs in some of the Grail stories

These fragments . . . ruins: the 'fragments' may describe the bits of quotations in the previous few lines or the whole of Eliot's poem. 'Shored' means piled up as a support and the 'ruins' could refer to the 'ruined tower' of the previous line or, in a more general way, to the chaos and waste he sees around him. 'Shore' can also mean to land from the sea and the Fisher King may be describing his catch

Why then . . . againe: 'Hieronymo's mad again' is the sub-title of *The Spanish Tragedy* (1594), a play by Thomas Kyd (1557–95). Hieronymo's son has been murdered and, unknown to the murderers, Hieronymo knows exactly what has happened. When asked by the murderers if he can help to entertain their fathers with a show, Hieronymo replies: 'Why then, Ile fit you. Say no more./When I was young, I gave my mind/And plied myself to fruitless poetry,/Which though it profit the professor naught/Yet is it passing pleasing to the world.'

Hieronymo sees his chance to gain his revenge and devises a play in which the parts, in different languages, are played by the people involved in his son's murder. While appearing to play-act he kills the murderers in front of their fathers. 'Ile fit you' seemed to mean, 'I shall cater for your wishes' but the knowingly 'mad' Hieronymo really means, 'I will give you what you deserve'

Datta. Dayadhvam. Damyata: (*Sanskrit*) Give. Sympathise. Control

Shantih shantih shantih: (*Sanskrit*) Eliot, in his note, informs us that the word repeated in this way marks a formal ending to an Upanishad. The Christian equivalent is: 'And the Peace of God, which passeth all understanding, shall keep your hearts and minds through Christ Jesus' (Philippians, 4:7)

Part 3

Commentary

Structure

One of the difficulties most people experience when they read *The Waste Land* for the first time is that they cannot see where the poem is going. The poem appears to belong to none of the main types of English poetry: it is not a narrative or dramatic or descriptive or lyric or meditative poem. These types have characteristic forms of organisation and development but *The Waste Land*, although it manifests certain elements of these types, does not demonstrate an immediately recognisable method of organisation. The reader may find that he understands individual lines or even whole sections but he does not see how they can fit together. Some critics have gone so far as to deny that *The Waste Land* is a poem at all, and T. S. Eliot himself had serious misgivings about the unity of the work even after he had reduced, with the help of Pound, what he called his 'sprawling chaotic poem'.

Undoubtedly, however, Eliot did have a method according to which he arranged the pieces of his poem. His arrangement or structure has much in common with the work of his contemporary artists in literature and other media (see pages 13–14). The parallel most helpful for our present discussion is that of film. A film consists of a sequence of photographs and the sequence is determined by the choice of the director who edits his total collection of photographs into a particular order. He can jump abruptly from one scene to another, introduce shots which go back in time behind the immediate action, even show shots from the future, present the dreams, fantasies and memories of characters. This process of arranging the shots is called 'montage'. In addition, the modern film director can manipulate not just the words of the characters but also sound effects to create atmosphere, evoke memories or arouse expectations. Eliot's method, in *The Waste Land*, of juxtaposing different pieces is very similar to the technique of montage. Such a technique allows the elements of the poem to act on the reader in an associative way even though he cannot see, in the initial stages, where he is being led. Gradually, as he reads on, certain themes, motifs, tones, even characters begin to develop through repetitions, echoes and similarities. As in an instrumental work of music the main tune or pattern of notes is hinted at, elaborated on and returned to; so, in *The Waste Land*, the central concerns of the poem impress themselves on the reader's mind.

There are several ways in which Eliot helps the reader to see the structure of his poem. In the first place, the poem is divided into five parts, each with a title which indicates the focus of the part, and each gathering together material appropriate to that focus. In Part I, Eliot outlines the problem of spiritual deadness. In Part II, he offers two particular examples of the mentality in the waste land which he expands on in Part III where he analyses the perversion of love. Part IV presents an alternative to the death by fire of Part III and indicates that this particular alternative is not a solution to the problem but merely a different sort of ending. In Part V the journey through the waste land is spelled out more clearly than before and the voice of the thunder suggests a remedy to cure the rottenness. This crude summary should not be taken as a description of a straightforward development; *The Waste Land* does not have a tidy plot.

One way in which a reader follows the progression in a poem is to attend to the central person involved, be he the narrator or a character: events and situations are seen in terms of this person. In *The Waste Land*, there does not appear to be such a figure. If the reader attaches himself to the 'I' in the poem, he quickly discovers that the 'I' is not the same person throughout. Eliot, aware of the problem, offers, in his note on line 218, what appears to be a solution. He writes: 'Tiresias, although a mere spectator and not indeed a "character", is yet the most important personage in the poem, uniting all the rest. Just as the one-eyed merchant, seller of currants, melts into the Phoenician Sailor, and the latter is not wholly distinct from Ferdinand, Prince of Naples, so all the women are one woman, and the two sexes meet in Tiresias. What Tiresias **sees**, in fact, is the substance of the poem.' This note is helpful in urging the reader to dispense with his wish for distinct and realistic characters and in emphasising that there is a mentality prevailing throughout the poem. The reader may well ask, however, how Tiresias is to be distinguished from the author and how, if so many seemingly diverse characters fuse into each other, Tiresias can be said to have any personality at all. During the period when he wrote *The Waste Land* (and the notes), Eliot was concerned that the poet should write impersonally: he, Tom Eliot, should not weep or laugh in a public poem. His note on the role of Tiresias should be taken seriously but not slavishly. The poem is the responsibility of the poet but, it must be stressed, the responsibility of reading the poem falls on the reader and in his mind the pieces must cohere. Each part of *The Waste Land* ends with an address to the reader: the hypocrite in Part I, the bystander at Ophelia's mad scene, the listener to the Fire Sermon, the voyager in

Part IV, and, by implication, still the hypocrite at the end of the poem. The poem's shape and meaning emerge in the reader's mind in so far as he is able to grasp them; **he** has to see 'the substance of the poem'.

A further way in which Eliot helps the reader to see an order in the poem is through his use of myth. He acknowledges his debt to Jessie Weston's *From Ritual to Romance* for suggesting 'the title, . . . the plan and a good deal of the incidental symbolism of the poem'. It may be that, as with Tiresias, Eliot alleges more than he fulfils but it is true that, throughout the poem, he establishes a network of references to the Grail legend and the vegetation rites closely associated with the legend. Vegetation rites are common to all societies and are so engrained in the human mind that, even if an individual reader is unacquainted with the stories of the Rhine gold, Thammuz or even the Fisher King, he can perceive enough of the fertility network in the poem to give him a sense of continuity. The legend of the Grail is further described on page 16.

Two elements in the poem which indicate a pattern are Eliot's use of allusion and his imagery and these will be discussed in the following pages. In *The Waste Land* they are not easily separable because Eliot takes his inspiration as much from his reading as from his direct experience.

Allusion

An allusion is an indirect reference made to something not immediately under discussion and a literary allusion is the inclusion in the work of one writer of quotations from, or reminders of, the work of another writer. No author writes in a vacuum and all authors show, in differing degrees, the influence of their reading but what the reader encounters in *The Waste Land* is the deliberate incorporation of Eliot's reading. Eliot's own attitude to this practice is made plain in his essays written in the years prior to 1922. In his essay on Philip Massinger (published in *The Sacred Wood*, 1920) he writes: 'Immature poets imitate; mature poets steal; bad poets deface what they take, and good poets make it into something better, or at least something different. The good poet welds his theft into a whole of feeling which is unique, utterly different from that from which it was torn; the bad poet throws it into something which has no cohesion.' He goes so far in 'Tradition and the Individual Talent' (1919) as to propose of the poet that 'we shall often find that not only the best, but the most individual parts of his work may be those in which the dead poets, his ancestors, assert their immortality most vigorously.' In his essay on the Metaphysical poets in 1921, he develops his point and asserts that 'Our civilisation comprehends great variety and complexity, and this variety and complexity, playing upon a refined sensibility, must produce various and complex results. The poet must become more and more comprehensive, more allusive, more indirect, in order to force, to dislocate if necessary language into his meaning.'

Eliot's concern with a cultural heritage, what he calls 'tradition', is central to all his work. In *The Waste Land* he uses allusions as evidence to show the permanent struggle of men to seek or reject truth. His technique, however, poses a number of problems for the reader. In the first place, how essential is it that an allusion be recognised? The answer must be that it varies from allusion to allusion. Some seem self-explanatory in their context in the poem; others seem to have no sense until their original context is known. In both cases, however, knowledge of the original context offers the possibility of a richer sense; otherwise, Eliot would be guilty of confusing the reader by expecting him to exclude from his mind the very associations triggered off by the allusion. The second question raised by the technique is: how much of the original context is being drawn on by the quotation of a single line or even a single word? If Eliot is fully in control of his poem the answer must be that the context in *The Waste Land* helps the reader to determine how much the allusion brings with it from its original context. One example will suffice to illustrate both questions. Line 259 begins 'O City city, . . .' The reader, arriving at this point, is aware that the City of London is one of the main locations used in the poem and could read line 259 without seeking any further sense or suspecting an allusion. On the other hand, he might detect a solemnity in this address to the City and might hear a connexion between this line and line 257 which, although it is a quotation from Shakespeare's *The Tempest*, links with the biblical line 182, 'By the waters of Leman I sat down and wept'. If these links are heard by him, he might well be reminded of Jesus weeping over the city of Jerusalem and when he consults St Matthew's account he finds that Jerusalem, like London, rejects the prophets and their wisdom. This reading of the line, elaborate as it sounds, is supported by the context and by the overall preoccupations of *The Waste Land*.

In the rich and varied allusiveness of the poem it is worth looking at some of the main sources for Eliot's allusions and asking why and how he uses them. The Bible is probably the single most pervasive influence on the poem. Throughout the Bible there is a series of prophetic voices which denounce the way in which the people and their rulers have deserted the true God and pursued false values. From early on (line 19) in *The Waste Land*, Eliot is similarly concerned to expose the decadence and spiritual emptiness of his own time and he invokes the biblical tone and turn of phrase, so recognisable to English speaking readers, to lend authority to his personal vision. Furthermore, the desolation and captivity brought on themselves by the folly of the Israelites offer a parallel to the story of the Fisher King, the Grail and the waste land. This parallel is developed in the obviously Christian element in the legend and by Eliot's introduction of the Hanged Man (Christ) and the journey to Emmaus where the resurrected saviour, sacrificed for the salvation of his people, goes unrecognised.

Dante and Baudelaire are used by Eliot to support his view of the modern city as a condition of horror. Dante's Hell and Purgatory (significantly, Eliot does not allude to his Paradise) are extensions of life and illuminations of it. Baudelaire presents the 'unreal city' directly in his poetry. Both Dante's and Baudelaire's poetry shows an acute awareness of the reader. Eliot harnesses their moral force to confront his reader with the death in life he sees all around him.

The allusions to Wagner's operas are explained in the notes and, for the reader who knows the operas referred to and their legends, the poem is enlarged by these echoes. Eliot is anxious to devise a poem of diverse materials and of wide suggestibility to appeal to different readers. Wagner's operas, exploring the perplexities and aspirations of men, themselves draw on their framework of ancient legends and myths and Eliot, in alluding to these complex operas, invites the reader to incorporate something of that complexity in his understanding of the poem.

Imagery

A poet when writing of ideas or feelings must, in order to avoid being too abstract, find terms which suggest the immediate, physical apprehension of these ideas and feelings; such terms are called images. The word 'imagery' is more generalised and is used to describe the strands of associative language used by a poet. In Shakespeare's play *Hamlet*, for example, there is imagery of corruption and disease running through the play, constantly reminding the reader of the immoral and therefore rotten state of affairs in the court of Denmark.

Imagery of sterility and dryness, appropriate to the condition of the waste land, is evident from the first few lines of the poem where the arrival of spring is viewed with horror by the inhabitants of the 'dead land'. They survive minimally in the 'strong rubbish' (line 20) under a relentless sun. This desert is not in contrast to the 'Unreal City' of line 60 for, in both, the people lack will and vitality. The same symptoms are manifested by the characters of Parts II and III and in the background the rattle of dead bones (lines 116, 186 and 194) mocks the futility and essential deadness of their lives. The desert landscape of Part I reappears in the final Part of the poem, in the section considered by Eliot himself to be the best written piece of *The Waste Land*. A change has taken place, however, in that the travellers through the lifeless sand and rock now crave for water and later, when tempted to despair in the 'empty cisterns and exhausted wells' of the ruined chapel, they reassure themselves that 'Dry bones can harm no one'. At the end, with the 'arid plain' behind him, the Fisher King, the ruler and embodiment of the waste land, faces the sea; behind him also are the polluted river and the dull canal, and now the rain intimated by the thunder offers new possibilities in place of the apprehension caused by the spring rain in line 4.

The frailty and corruption of human love is largely presented in images of sexual degradation. Even in the episode of the hyacinth girl with all its marvellous promise there is a sudden inability to communicate, a sense of sexual inadequacy. In a less intense way, the two relationships explored in Part II reiterate the failure of men and women to achieve a partnership of mutual trust and care. The title of Part II, 'A Game of Chess' (see note, page 26), emphasises the theme of deceit and sexual exploitation and 'The Fire Sermon', concerned as it is with burning, focuses on the fires of sexual lust. The 'sweet Thames' becomes the 'waters of Leman' or prostitution and Eliot is determined to demonstrate how disgusting and depraved men can become in the waste land. Women are reduced to sexual objects for the gratification of lust and they seem to accept tamely the mechanical role they are given to play. Dignity and honour are not considered any longer: 'She smooths her hair with automatic hand,' and, 'What should I resent?' In the final part, however, in the responses to the voice of the thunder, there is a questioning of the selfish lust which had motivated the characters earlier in the poem; in particular, the sailing image of control and sharing counteracts the images of Philomel, Cleopatra, Dido, Queen Elizabeth and the other women.

A third strand of imagery communicates Eliot's fascination with the transformation of life into death and death into life. At the beginning of the poem the inhabitants of the 'dead land' are barely alive and in line 63, the poet expresses his surprise that 'death had undone so many'. In the final lines of Part I, however, there is some hope offered that the buried corpse may begin to grow. The Egyptian myth of Osiris (see note on page 24) symbolised the dying of the land and its rebirth with the rising of the water in the Nile. Throughout the poem there is an uncertainty about the distinction between life and death: corpses can sprout but those who seem to be alive are sometimes 'neither/living nor dead' (lines 39–40) or are asked, 'Are you alive, or not?' (line 126). This paradox of death in life is seen most acutely in the story of Jesus (lines 328–330) who, as god and man, had lived most fully but appeared to be killed on the cross. Jesus, however, epitomises the myths of the sacrificed but resurrected god of fertility and he reappears to his followers and offers a new life. Earlier in the poem, Eliot cites many examples of transformation in people's lives, some suggesting an improvement, some indicating a deterioration or confusion. Philomel, transformed into a bird, is a plaintive reminder of the brutality of human life. Even Tiresias who has experienced so much as male and female, appears to be, like the Cumaean Sybil of the epigraph, weary of all behaviour. Phlebas's death by water merely involves him in a repetition of his life: he does not escape from the wheel. On the other hand, the references to Ariel's song in Shakespeare's *The Tempest* allow that death by drowning may lead to 'something rich and strange', and St Augustine and the Buddha, when they are rescued from their burning condition, point to a fuller kind of living.

Style

Since the poem appeared in 1922, many readers have been impressed with Eliot's versatility in using different verse forms and in varying the tone. Part of his success comes from his competence in mimicking the style of other writers and even incorporating quotations from them; and part also stems from his ability to modulate the pace and seriousness of his poem. In a consideration of the effect of a poem, verse and language cannot, ultimately, be separated but, at this stage, for the sake of brevity and clarity, it is easier to look at each in turn.

Verse

The lack of a sustained metrical form in *The Waste Land* led some readers to conclude that Eliot had smashed the traditional rules of verse and that he wrote in free verse. The poet himself, however, declared that no worthwhile verse can ever be called free because the poet is always in control of his resources. It is true that there is no consistent metre (or pattern of stressed syllables) running through the poem, and the number of syllables in a line varies from one to seventeen; some lines and sections have rhyme and others do not; and, in places, Eliot does not use punctuation marks in the conventional way. Nonetheless, he does employ one or more of such devices in different sections of the poem to give an impression of flexible but ordered verse, and it is part of the reader's pleasure in the poem to follow Eliot from the extreme of casual conversation, as in the pub, to the extreme of mechanical nursery rhyme (line 426).

In the opening seven lines of the poem, the basic measure is the line of four stressed syllables but what holds the lines together is Eliot's use of the verbs in the present participle at the end of the lines, sounding like a rhyme, but always needing the next line to complete the sense: a momentum and suspense are created. The following lines sound more casual, a mere sequence of movements, until Marie describes her sled ride and then the short phrases, the alternation of 'we', 'he' and 'I', the repetition of her name, the heavy stress on 'down' (line 16), all contribute to communicate her breathless anxiety.

The first seventeen lines of 'A Game of Chess' consist of two sentences. Rhyme is not used but the stress pattern is reminiscent of Shakespearean blank verse. The syntax in both sentences is intricate and the lines run on into the next with the result that the reader has difficulty in keeping his control of the sense. This confusion is increased by Eliot's use of past tenses of verbs which can often also serve as adjectives, for example, 'burnished', 'glowed', 'held up', 'wrought', 'fruited' in the first three lines.

A totally different example of Eliot's handling of verse can be seen in the episode concerning the typist (lines 215–256). Rhyme occurs in most of the lines although not according to any rigid scheme. In many of the lines the rhyme on a stressed syllable emphasises the unit of the line and the action of the scene progresses line by line in a mechanical, monotonous way. Sometimes the rhymes are so neat and obvious that they mock the actions; this effect is most noticeable when a shorter word is joined by rhyme with a longer one, for example, 'one bold stare' and 'millionaire', 'defence' and 'indifference', and 'alone' and 'gramophone'.

The description of the journey through the desert in Part V (lines 331–358) has no marks of punctuation and a reading of the passage depends heavily on Eliot's manipulation of the line and his use of repetitions and parallel phrases. 'Water' occurs eleven times, 'rock' nine times, 'mountains' five times and the five conditional clauses beginning with 'if' are answered by five statements beginning with 'but'. The repetitions, the lack of punctuation and the negation emphasise an unending, unprogressing, nightmarish journey; the reader longs for relief, an exit from the labyrinth.

In the course of the poem, Eliot exploits to the full the possibilities of verse based on the stress patterns of conversational English, now tightening, now relaxing the tension. Rhyme is employed to round off a section or emphasise a point. Even in the most casual passages such as the conversation in the pub, the poet formalises the speech by making most lines complete in themselves, repeating 'she said' or 'I said' almost like a rhyme and introducing the refrain, 'Hurry up please its time'.

Language

In the sections on allusion and imagery, Eliot's choice of language has already been discussed, but something has to be said about his variety of tone and his shifts in vocabulary. *The Waste Land* is a dramatic poem featuring many characters and many scenes. 'He do the police in different voices', the original title of the poem, offers a clue to Eliot's method of juxtaposing characters and scenes, sometimes for the sake of contrast, more commonly to demonstrate the common fate of all men.

In Part I, after the solemn tone of lines 19–30, derived from the prophetic books of the Bible, Eliot introduces the lyrical intensity of the episode with the hyacinth girl. The man is caught in an emotional paralysis where he can neither speak nor see nor even feel conscious. His condition of helplessness is followed by the description of Madame Sosostris, 'famous clairvoyante'. A clairvoyante is a person who, often in a state of trance, sees what is not present. Madame Sosostris seems to be a direct contrast to the blinded lover but Eliot presents her in such an ironic manner that she emerges as a comic parallel to the man. Her name (see page 22) suggests her bogus status and Eliot immediately undercuts her reputation as a 'famous clairvoyante' by telling the reader that she 'had a bad cold'. In the following lines, with a similar irony, 'wisest' is contradicted by 'wicked'.

A similar shift of moods and tone is apparent in the opening thirty-three lines of 'The Fire Sermon'. Eliot, first of all, presents alongside each other the gentle grace of Spenser's world and the vulgar details of the modern scene. The refrain, 'Sweet Thames, run softly till I end my song' comes to communicate an elegiac mood, a sense of regret. This mood is disrupted by the introduction of 'bones', 'chuckle', 'rat', 'slimy belly' but reappears briefly when the narrator muses on the death of his father and brother. Eliot allows no mood or tone to prevail for long and his lines on Mrs Porter bring an incongruous comic touch to the section. The placing of the French quotation is obviously intended to act in the reader's mind as a comment on Mrs Porter and her crudity, but the pure voices of the children in the chapel are given new words to sing in the lines immediately following.

Such shifts and juxtapositions occur throughout the entire poem: they constitute the texture of the poem. Ornate vocabulary gives way to colloquial dialogue, lyrical moments are interrupted by sordid intrusions, the comic and the macabre coexist with the solemn words of religious instruction, one language is supplanted by another, until in the final lines of the poem the fragments are collected together.

Meaning

Since the poem appeared in 1922 there have been many contradictory reactions to it. Some readers have considered it to be an intellectual puzzle devised for such people as enjoy crossword puzzles. Some have dismissed it as a joke against academic critics and have seen Eliot's notes as his final trick. Some have assessed it as the finest example of modernist art, reflecting in its own difficulties the complexity of the modern world. Some have heard in the poem a whimper of despair. Some have sensed that behind the cleverness of the poem a tortured lover was seeking to justify himself. The theories, interpretations and assessments are amazingly diverse and this fact has led some critics to admire the poem that can stimulate so many reactions. Others have been suspicious about a work in which so much is unclear.

Eliot's own comments have not helped to elucidate the problems posed by *The Waste Land*, partly because his own attitude to the poem changed over the years. Originally, readers in the 1920s were encouraged by Eliot's theories of poetry advanced in his essays to believe that the poem was an impersonal object but, later in his life, Eliot described it as a 'wholly insignificant grouse against life; . . . a piece of rhythmical grumbling'. In 1932 Eliot wrote: 'When I wrote a poem called *The Waste Land* some of the more approving critics said I had expressed "the disillusion of a generation", which is nonsense. I may have expressed for them their own illusion of being disillusioned, but that did not form part of my intention'. In 1951, however, he asserted that, 'A poet may believe that he is expressing only his private experience; his lines may be for him only a means of talking about himself without giving himself away; yet for his readers what he has written may come to be the expression both of their own secret feelings and of the exultation or despair of a generation'. What is undoubtedly clear, whatever Eliot felt he had intended or disguised, is that certain obsessions, habits of temperament and attitudes are discernible in the choice of incident and image. Eliot's concern with blighted sexuality is too persistent to be considered incidental or contrived: it has the urgency of an unsolved personal problem.

To acknowledge a personal foundation in the poem is not to undermine the whole construction. The view of life presented in the poem is narrowed by the peculiar bias of the author but, by fusing his personal element into the larger story of the Grail and the fertility myths and offering some possibilities beyond his own condition, Eliot succeeds in persuading the reader that such a view has a wider validity. Mention of other possibilities raises the question which has vexed critics: does the poem contain a progression? The first three parts examine the spiritual sickness of the waste land and in the final part, after the journey to the Chapel of the Grail is completed, the voice of the thunder offers a diagnosis. Lacking the capacity to give, man is unable to live in any worthwhile sense. How can he discover this capacity? Eliot seems uncertain as to how to proceed. After the commands of the thunder have been interpreted and the lack of genuine giving has been conceded, the poem concludes with a series of apparently contradictory statements and the eventual blessing (see page 42). Thus, Eliot does indicate the direction of a progression and he has shown what has caused the sterility of the waste land; what he does not present (and it is probable that he could not at this stage in his life) is a demonstration of a regeneration. Eliot, like the tormented Hieronymo, understands his situation and can dare to hope. The reader familiar with the poet's later work, where his individual regeneration is explored, can see the journey through the waste land as a hard stage towards the Christian solution he eventually found. Eliot, in *The Waste Land* and his other works, sees the human condition in religious terms and shows little understanding of the economic and social pressures on men. There is little evidence of a sympathetic view of human frailty. Eliot's use of literary allusion and ancient myth tends to confirm the opinion that he sees his fellow men from a distance.

In his critical essays, Eliot asserts that enjoyment precedes interpretation for the reader of poetry. Even for a reader who is antipathetic to what seems to be Eliot's view of his generation or human nature, *The Waste Land* offers a great deal of pleasure. It has proved to be a most memorable poem full of wit, sharp insights, unusual perspective, haunting rhythms, suggested depths and sad images of apathy and lovelessness. The poem's enduring popularity and its enormous influence on poets in many languages provide evidence that, for many readers throughout the world, it touches a nerve, it prompts a recognition, it presents, not necessarily **the** truth, but a truth about man's failures and aspirations.

Part 4

Hints for study

(a) Read the poem aloud many times over a period of days or weeks. Make no special effort to understand local difficulties but allow the poem to speak for itself. The sound and nature, the 'feel', of the poem should enter your mind. When you read, pay careful attention to the different combinations of line length, punctuation, rhythm, rhyme and intonation used by Eliot. Hear in your own reading the different voices of the poem.

(b) Because of Eliot's use of past writers and his wish that the reader should recognise these past writers, you should be familiar with the actual nature of the more prominent of such writers. It is suggested, therefore, that you read the following: Dante, *Hell*, Cantos 1–5; The Bible, Ezekiel, Chapters 1–3; any poems of Baudelaire included in an anthology of French verse; Webster, *The White Devil*, Act 5; and Shakespeare, *The Tempest*, Act 1.

(c) Write brief summaries of each section of the poem. *The Waste Land* is not a story, so summaries can merely indicate what is going on in the poem. To make yourself write such summaries, however, is to force you to attend to the general order of the poem and impress it on your mind.

(d) Make a list of the characters in the poem and write short descriptions of them. Again, these characters are not like the characters in a play or a novel but the differences and similarities between the figures devised by Eliot are an essential part of the nature of the poem. Consider, also, the identity of the 'I', 'we' and 'you' in the poem.

(e) Take random passages of a dozen lines and observe Eliot's juxtapositions of action, character, historical period, vocabulary and tone. Try to work out how they function together.

(f) Choose passages of a similar length and ascertain how the rhythm, line, punctuation and rhyme are handled and relate these elements to the sense.

(g) When you enjoy a passage or a line, make a point of learning it by heart. Such pieces maintain the actuality of the poem in your mind and help you to guard against seeing the poem solely in terms of ideas.

(*h*) Remind yourself that the nature of *The Waste Land* does not demand that you can trace every single allusion or reference. On the other hand, avoid the arrogance of asserting that anything unfamiliar to you is therefore unimportant.

(ii) Quotations appropriate to particular topics

In any spoken or written discussion of the poem, certain topics are likely to be raised. Many of the major topics have already been dealt with in the Commentary section but some additional ones are listed here and the lines relevant to them are indicated.

(*a*) **The city.** (The modern city and the desert are the main locations of the poem. It seems that, for Eliot, the modern city is the appropriate setting for the spiritual illness he identifies.)

line 56 (Madame Sosostris sees the futile life of men in cities); lines 60–68 (description of crowds of dull people going to work in London); lines 131–138 (the monotonous, empty life of the rich); lines 139–172 (scene of working class women in a London pub); the whole of 'The Fire Sermon' takes place in the city; lines 371–376 (vision of the destruction of great urban civilisations).

(*b*) **Lyrical element.** (Moments of heightened emotion which help to balance the prevailing dullness described in the poem.)

lines 1–7 (expresses fear of the stirring of the lyrical impulse by spring); lines 31–42 (poignant episode of the hyacinth girl in the frame of the love story of Tristan and Isolde); lines 99–103 (tragic story of Philomel in the beautiful song of the nightingale); line 202 (the pure voices of the children in the chapel of the Grail); lines 257–265 (the bright moment at the church of Magnus Martyr); lines 279–289 (a suggestion of a finer beauty); lines 402–404 (moment of ecstasy); lines 418–422 (promise of shared pleasure); line 428 (cry of longing).

(c) **Elegiac element.** (Conveying a sense of loss and regret.)

lines 1-7 (looking back to the comfort of not feeling anything); lines 35-42 (sadness of unfulfilled promise); line 48 (line from the song of lament and consolation in *The Tempest*); lines 63-65 (dismay at how death has entered into the living); lines 97-103 (sad fate of Philomel); lines 124-125 (compare line 48); line 172 (Ophelia's line of farewell from *Hamlet*); lines 173-184 (lament for lost beauty and innocence); lines 191-192 (dead relatives); lines 253-256 (mocking regret); line 259 (sad form of address); lines 277-306 (lament of the Thames and Rhine maidens); lines 312-321 (elegy for the drowned Phlebas); lines 322-330 (loss of the saviour); line 367 (universal lament); lines 383-388 (nothing but memories and decay); lines 406-409 (all that remains of the dead).

(d) **Macabre element.** (Eliot shows a fascination with death, physical unpleasantness and the unnatural.)

line 30 (image of death); line 52; line 55; lines 62-65 (death in life); lines 71-75 (the planted corpse and the eager dog); lines 99-110 (the raped and tongueless Philomel is only one of the ghostly figures haunting the room where nothing is natural); lines 115-116 (dead bones and rats); line 138 ('lidless eyes'); lines 144-146 (ugly Lil with rotten teeth); lines 156-161 (unnatural looks and abortion); lines 185-195 (images of death, decay and nastiness); lines 218-219 (blind Tiresias of mixed sex); line 231 (clerk has unhealthy skin); line 303; lines 315-316 (Phlebas is decomposing); line 339 (rottenness); lines

359–365 (ghostly, unknown figure); lines 377–390 (unnatural happenings like those in a nightmare); lines 406–409 (death and decay); lines 411–413 (the horrible story of Ugolino and his family); line 431 (mad Hieronymo and his story).

(e) **Religious element.** (Aspects of the Grail legend run through the poem but there are also specific references to Christianity, eastern religions and the fertility rituals of older religions.)

lines 19–30 (voice of the prophets of the Bible); lines 35–41 (related to sacred place in a fertility rite); lines 43–59 (Madame Sosostris is an example of the false prophet); lines 71–75 (fertility ritual connected with Osiris); line 182 (captivity of the Hebrews); line 202 (purification in the Chapel Perilous); lines 263–265 (mystery of church atmosphere); lines 277–278 (Rhine-maidens were sacred); lines 307–311 (Augustine and the Buddha); line 319 (all mankind, according to the Bible); lines 322–330 (arrest and crucifixion of Jesus); lines 359–365 (the resurrected Jesus); lines 385–392 (arrival at the Chapel Perilous and the new day); lines 395–399 (holy places of Indian religions); lines 400–401, 410–411, 417–418 (voice of the thunder of God); lines 432–433 (final religious command and blessing).

(iii) Answering questions on poetry

(a) Examine the particular question carefully. Make sure that you understand the wording of the question and what kind of answer it requires. Many questions assume certain values; you may feel that you have to challenge these implied values.

(b) Plan your answer. Devote your first paragraph to discussing the question and providing any necessary background material. Determine what are to be the main points in your answer, remembering that evidence from the poem is needed to support your argument. You are trying to persuade the examiner that your view of the poem (and of the question) is justified. Your essay should end with a brief conclusion showing what you have proved.

(c) Quotations are needed to demonstrate that what you assert about the poem is true. Quotations also give the actual flavour of the poem in a manner which you cannot describe.

(d) The nature of the poetry should be made evident in your discussion. If the poem is comic or lyrical or dramatic such a quality must be conveyed in your answer. The overall shape and texture of the poem should be implied in your answer.

(e) Avoid abstract words unless they are absolutely necessary. Write clearly and directly.

(f) Do not repeat the ideas, interpretations or special vocabulary of critics until you are fully persuaded of their validity and have assimilated them.

(g) Remember that the poem is separated from its author by being published and his opinions on it may be interesting or helpful but, eventually, the poem is as he published it. It must explain itself; it belongs to the readers. Certainly know about the author's life, his period and his other works but do not add biographical or background material unless it is strictly relevant to the literary question.

(iv) Plan for a sample answer to a question

Question: It has been suggested that *The Waste Land* is organised like a piece of music. Discuss the part played by music in the poem.

Answer: Introduction. The two sentences of the question do not overlap as completely as appears at first glance. The first sentence talks about the organisation of the poem; the second asks about any aspect of music evident in the poem. The first sentence seems to assume that a piece of music is organised in a specific, recognisable way. Is this a reasonable assumption? Surely there are different kinds of organisation? Generally speaking, however, western music is organised round a theme (or tune or set of notes) and the musical piece develops through variations on this theme. Some conflict or interplay takes place between the variations and eventually a resolution is reached. The musical piece is held together by echoes and repetitions of the theme, and of motifs reminding the reader of particular moods or instruments. Does such an organisation occur in *The Waste Land*?

MAIN POINTS

(1) Is a theme, in the musical sense, presented at the beginning of the poem? There is no one place where the essence of the poem is stated although some sections (for example, lines 1–7 and lines 19–24) propose what comes to be seen in retrospect as central concerns of the whole poem. The theme, in both a musical and a literary sense, develops more gradually and, when it does develop, is more concrete than a musical theme can be.

(2) Are there variations on a theme? Granted that the theme develops differently, it can be seen that the whole poem consists of variations on a central view of life. Parts II and III offer a series of characters and incidents and the sterility and futility of the waste land are made apparent through them. Irrespective of social class or money, the lives shown have the same spiritual deadness. The pace and mood are varied in the different sections of the poem but not in the large-scale way of the movements in, for example, a symphonic composition. Eliot does, in the last section, offer the possibility of an escape from the routine he has shown but the ending of the poem is deliberately unclear. The variations are not fully resolved.

(3) Are echoes and motifs used? Through the imagery of the entire poem and the repeated lines an effect not unlike that of a piece of music is created. For example, the repetion of 'dead' or 'death' sounds through the poem from 'the dead land' (line 2), 'the dead tree' (line 23), 'neither/ living nor dead' (lines 39–40), 'I had not thought death had undone so many' (line 63), 'Where dead men lost their bones' (line 116), 'Phlebas the Phoenician, a fortnight dead' (line 312) to 'He who was living is now dead' (line 328). The word 'unreal' in line 60 recurs in lines 207 and 376. In the pub scene in Part II the line 'Hurry up please its time' occurs like a refrain five times. References to Philomel come in Parts II, III and V, insisting that the reader's mind should not forget.

(4) Music in the poem. Eliot incorporates many references to songs, singing birds and musical instruments in *The Waste Land*. Often he employs them to signal a mood as in his use of the lines from Wagner's *Tristan and Isolde* and Ariel's song from *The Tempest*. The Shakespeherian Rag of lines 128–130 and the 'record on the gramophone' in line 256 are dull sounds in comparison with the mandoline in line 261. A similar contrast is set up between the vulgar song about Mrs Porter and the line immediately following describing the voices of the boys singing in the Chapel Perilous. Wagner's lament of the Rhine-maidens is used to strengthen the picture of modern corruption on the Thames. Eliot uses musical sounds to vary the appeal of his poem: the 'horns and motors' (line 197) are a parody of Actaeon's hunting horns; the 'fiddled

whisper music' (line 378) is a surrealistic touch; the line from 'London Bridge', an old song now sung by children, provides one of the incongruous fragments at the end of the poem.

CONCLUSION·

Music is an important element in *The Waste Land* both in references made to musical sounds and in certain similarities between the organisation of a piece of music and Eliot's poem. To press the analogy too far would be a mistake because a poem made with words is bound to be different from a musical composition. Also, the idea of a musical theme cannot operate as such in a poem and to talk about one art form in terms of another is usually to confuse both.

(v) Questions

(1) What do you understand to be the main themes of *The Waste Land*?

(2) Write an analysis of the episode involving the typist and the clerk in 'The Fire Sermon.' Show also in what ways the episode is related to the rest of the poem.

(3) Write an essay discussing Eliot's use of images of dryness and water in *The Waste Land*.

(4) Discuss the first paragraph (lines 1–18) of 'The Burial of the Dead' as an introductory paragraph to the poem.

(5) How far does the reader need to recognise the source of Eliot's allusions in *The Waste Land*?

(6) Using a number of examples, show how Eliot uses rhyme in *The Waste Land*.

(7) In what ways does the message of the thunder relate to the earlier parts of the poem?

(8) 'Tiresias, although a mere spectator and not indeed a "character", is yet the most important personage in the poem, uniting all the rest.' How helpful do you find Eliot's note on Tiresias?

(9) Write a comparison of the two scenes in 'A Game of Chess', paying attention to style as well as content.

(10) In what sense can *The Waste Land* be described as 'a religious poem'? Do you consider the religious element to be significant?

(11) Discuss Eliot's use of the past, historical and literary, in *The Waste Land*.

(12) Attempt to justify Eliot's method in *The Waste Land*.

(13) Explain the meaning of the titles, 'The Burial of the Dead' and 'The Fire Sermon' and show how they function in their parts of the poem.

(14) What is the function of the Grail Legend in the organisation and general meaning of *The Waste Land*?

(15) In what senses can *The Waste Land* be described as a dramatic poem?

(16) Is there a progression in *The Waste Land*?

(17) Why do you think sexual relationships are given such a prominent place in the poem? Discuss Eliot's treatment of sexual relationships.

(18) '*The Waste Land* presents too persistently gloomy a picture of life to justify its reputation as a major poem.' Discuss.

(19) Does Madame Sosostris's reading of the Tarot cards provide any help to our understanding of the poem?

(20) Is 'Death by Water' necessary to the poem? Discuss the justifications for its inclusion.

(21) Choose four examples of repeated words or phrases and show how Eliot uses the repetition in the poem.

(22) Attempt to explain the final eleven lines of the poem. Do they provide a satisfactory ending to the poem?

(23) Is it possible to decide whether or not *The Waste Land* presents 'the disillusionment of a generation'?

Part 5

Suggestions for further reading

Text of the poem

ELIOT, T. S.: *The Complete Poems and Plays of T. S. Eliot*, Faber and Faber, London, 1969

ELIOT, VALERIE, (ED.): *The Waste Land: A Facsimile and Transcripts of the Original Drafts*, Faber and Faber, London, 1971

Other works by T. S. Eliot

ELIOT, T. S.: *Selected Essays*, third edition, Faber and Faber, London, 1951. Particularly recommended are the essays on 'Tradition and the Individual Talent' (1919); 'Hamlet' (1919); 'Philip Massinger' (1920); 'The Metaphysical Poets' (1921); 'Andrew Marvell' (1921); 'Dante' (1929); and 'Baudelaire' (1930)

Books on T. S. Eliot

BRADBROOK, M. C.: *T. S. Eliot*, revised edition, Longmans, London, 1965. Short, clear introduction to Eliot, a British Council pamphlet in the Writers and their Work series

HOWARTH, HERBERT: *Notes on Some Figures Behind T. S. Eliot*, Chatto and Windus, London, 1965. Informative, particularly on the poet's education and reading

MATTHIESSEN, F. O.: *The Achievement of T. S. Eliot*, third edition, Oxford University Press, London, 1958. Intelligent and sympathetic but quite difficult

SMITH, GROVER: *T. S. Eliot's Poetry and Plays: A Study in Sources and Meaning*, second edition, University of Chicago Press, Chicago, 1974. Very thorough but occasionally insensitive and misleading

SPENDER, STEPHEN: *Eliot*, Collins/Fontana, London, 1975. Readable and comprehensive study of Eliot

STEAD, C. K.: *The New Poetic*, Hutchinson, London, 1964. Interesting on Eliot's theories and his connexions with other modern poets

Books on *The Waste Land*

BRADBROOK, M. C.: *T. S. Eliot: The Making of The Waste Land*, Longman, London, 1972. Short British Council pamphlet examining the manuscripts of the poem

COX, C. B., AND HINCHLIFFE, ARNOLD P. (EDS.): *T. S. Eliot: The Waste Land*, Macmillan, London, 1968. Includes comments by Eliot, early reviews, and some of the best criticism of the poem

MARTIN, JAY, (ED.): *A Collection of Critical Essays on The Waste Land*, Prentice-Hall, Eaglewood Cliffs, New Jersey, 1968. A different selection of critical views from that of the previous book

The author of these notes

ALASDAIR D. F. MACRAE was educated at the University of Edinburgh and taught for a short time in secondary schools before taking up a lectureship in the University of Khartoum, Republic of the Sudan. He is now lecturer in English Studies at the University of Stirling. He is at present engaged in work on the modern poet Edwin Muir and the poetry of Shelley. He is the author of the York Notes on *Macbeth*.

YORK NOTES

The first 200 titles